# THE HANDBOOK OF
# GLIDER
# AEROBATICS

# THE HANDBOOK OF
# GLIDER
# AEROBATICS

PETER MIKE
MALLINSON & WOOLLARD

**Airlife**
England

First published in the UK in 1999
by Airlife Publishing Ltd

**British Library Cataloguing-in-Publication Data**
  A catalogue record for this book
  is available from the British Library

ISBN 1 84037 110 2

Printed in England by Bath Press, Bath.

**Airlife Publishing Ltd**
101 Longden Road, Shrewsbury, SY3 9EB, England
E-mail: airlife@airlifebooks.com
Website: www.airlifebooks.com

# Contents

# Acknowledgements

No instructional book of this kind can be assembled without the combined experience and knowledge of a host of contributors, no matter how small or even unwitting their input may have seemed. To all those who have helped, we owe a debt of sincerest gratitude.

We would like to thank the many specialists and aerobatic pilots without whose advice and scrutinies we hardly dare think of the more grievous errors we might have made. In particular Guy Westgate, who has helped greatly with the final drafting, content and proof-reading, and has also supplied many of the photographs used, including that on the cover. Also, Lionel Sole, Colin Short, Sam Mummery, Frank Irving, John Gilbert, Jim Duthie, Ray Stoward, the late Ted Lysakowski and Simon Larkin, to name but a few. A similar service has been provided most generously by all those friends and instructors who have taken so much trouble over checking the multitude of drafts which have flowed from the printer.

We are also indebted to Kay and Mike Balmforth and Linda Bassett of The Image Works, Advertising and Design Consultancy, Kenton, Exeter, who have so generously given their professional skills and advice and put their layout and graphics technology at our disposal, and to Wendy Durham of Gradient PR for the final preparation.

Finally, without the introduction to aerobatic flying by the Polish champion Joseph Solski, the seeds from which this book has grown might never have been sown. His inspirational instruction and compelling manner, with his modest command of the English language, is an object lesson to Flying Instructors everywhere.

**P**eter Mallinson and Mike Woollard both started flying gliders at Nympsfield in Gloucestershire in their late 20s and their flying careers progressed along parallel paths. They both spread their wings to include powered aviation at an early stage and were soon flying a Fournier RF4D motor glider. This aeroplane with its delightful aerobatic qualities undoubtedly encouraged them in their common fascination for aerobatics. In 1989 they attended a course in glider aerobatics run by the Polish champion, Joseph Solski and were instantly inspired by his remarkable flying and instructing skills.

## Peter Mallinson

**P**eter is a Research Zoologist by profession although with an initial engineering background. He describes his lifelong love of flying as 'genetic', although he wonders whether it may have been influenced by his childhood environment as the son of an RAF pilot.

He started flying in 1977 at the age of 28 at Nympsfield, which remains his home club. He sees aerobatics as a natural progression in the process of learning to fly aeroplanes and launched seriously into aerobatics following the 1989 course. He has travelled extensively in

Poland and Germany pursuing further training and after seeing the advanced state of the sport on the continent has been determined to promote the sport of Glider Aerobatics in the UK. He has spent many hours teaching aerobatics at Nympsfield and other clubs around the country and was appointed BGA Regional Aerobatic Examiner in 1995.

## Mike Woollard

**M**ike is a Chartered Mechanical Engineer with a deep rooted and professional interest in aerodynamic and technical matters related to aviation. He is Chairman of the British Gliding Association Technical Committee. He started gliding at Nympsfield in 1980 at the age of 27, moving in 1992 to the Cambridge Gliding Club at Gransden Lodge. He holds a BGA Advanced Aerobatic Instructor's rating. Much of his aerobatic flying experience has been gained 'hanging in the straps' of various aerobatic two-seater training gliders in which he regularly instructs, or in his favourite aerobatic practice mounts, the RF4D and the Fox.

He is also a keen cross-country pilot, flying a Standard Cirrus glider which he shares with his wife Susan.

# About this Book

This book provides a reference point for use in conjunction with aerobatic instruction. It aims to provide an understanding of the important subjects that are essential for safe and successful aerobatic flying. However, no amount of reading can ever be a substitute for practical flying instruction and this is never more so than with aerobatics. None of the techniques described in this book should be attempted without proper training or check flights with a suitably qualified Aerobatic Instructor. The authors would like to point out that they can in no way be held responsible for any incorrect interpretation of any subject or technique described in this book, although every attempt has been made to present clear and unambiguous information.

The book has been divided into two main sections and an appendix.

## Section A: Theory

deals with the following four topics...
1 **Safety Considerations**
2 **Flight Envelopes**
3 **Glider Design**
4 **Aresti**

## Section B: Flying the Figures

describes in general terms how to fly some of the figures most commonly encountered. There are eleven figures from the beginners or 'Standard' level and nine from the more advanced levels.

The techniques described in Section B are necessarily generalised, since they will vary according to glider type. It is therefore essential to check with flight manuals and experienced aerobatic pilots for the appropriate speeds and techniques for specific gliders and any effect cockpit weight variations may have.

## Appendix

includes a step-by-step guide to constructing Flight Envelopes for various gliders.

# Glossary of Symbols

| | |
|---|---|
| $\alpha$ | Angle of attack of the wing |
| ASI | Airspeed indicator |
| BAeA | British Aerobatic Association |
| C of G | Centre of gravity |
| CGT | Centre of gravity track |
| $C_L$ | Coefficient of lift |
| g | Acceleration loading measured in gravitational units |
| JAR22 | Joint Airworthiness Requirement for Sailplanes & Motor Gliders |
| K | Aresti difficulty factor for aerobatic figures |
| n | Load factor on airframe in multiples of g |
| $n_1$ | Positive load factor at maximum manoeuvring speed |
| $n_2$ | Positive load factor at design maximum speed for erect flight |
| $n_3$ | Negative load factor at design maximum speed for inverted flight |
| $n_4$ | Negative load factor at the inverted maximum manoeuvring speed |
| QFE | Height relative to local ground elevation |
| V | Velocity |
| $V_a$ | Maximum manoeuvring speed |
| $V'_a$ | Inverted max manoeuvring speed |
| $V_{ne}$ | Velocity never exceed in erect flight |
| $V'_{ne}$ | Velocity never exceed in inverted flight |
| $V_{s1}$ | Erect stalling speed |
| $V'_{s1}$ | Inverted stalling speed |
| $V_{df}$ | Maximum flight test speed |
| $V_d$ | Design maximum speed |
| $V_b$ | Maximum rough air speed |
| ZLA | Zero lift axis (of fuselage) |

TOP: Tail view of the Lö 100 (foreground) and Fox-MDM-1 (background). (*Guy Westgate*)
ABOVE: Pilatus B4-PC11A 'Unlimited' aerobatic glider. (*Guy Westgate*)

TOP:  Keeping a Fox pilot cool before a competition flight. (*Guy Westgate*)
ABOVE:  Swift S1 on the approach and another preparing to launch (foreground). (*Guy Westgate*)

# Why Aerobatics?

**M**ost pilots who want to learn aerobatics will at some time find themselves asking this question. What exactly is it they want to achieve? What is it about aerobatics that is so fascinating, so compelling? They will probably find many answers.

For some it may simply be the thrill and exhilaration of flying the manœuvres. For others there will be an irresistible challenge in flying pre-defined figures to a strict set of criteria which will relentlessly test and develop their skill. Many pilots comment on the boost to general flying confidence which aerobatic training can give, often with particular reference to coping with unusual situations and attitudes.

Whatever reasons there may be, there can be little doubt that aerobatic training deepens our understanding of the flight characteristics of a glider and develops our ability to explore its capabilities. In aerobatics we are learning to perform standard figures as accurately and safely as possible and to combine them in sequences known as aerobatic programmes.

Like any challenge, learning aerobatics will be frustrating at times, but ultimately the sense of achievement and elation that follows from a well flown programme is worth every ounce of effort and determination. Few would disagree that well performed aerobatics are a joy for the pilot to fly as well as a beauty for the observer to behold.

The learning process for aerobatics requires a number of essential ingredients . . .

- **An understanding of all safety considerations**
- **An understanding of the theory**
- **Proper tuition**
- **A disciplined approach**
- **Practice, with observation from the ground**

# Section A: Theory

This section covers the following four topics . . .

1 **Safety Considerations**
2 **Flight Envelopes**
3 **Glider Design**
4 **Aresti**

All aspiring aerobatic pilots should have a sound knowledge and understanding of these topics as the foundation of their aerobatic flight training.

## 1 Safety Considerations

Safety is placed at the top of the list deliberately and you will find it frequently emphasised. In any form of flying there are so many safety considerations that they can seem almost too numerous to list. Fortunately, many of them are obvious and quickly become second nature, while others we have constantly to remind ourselves about. There are also a few which are not obvious at all, but may be equally important.

In aerobatics we are often flying much closer to the design limits of an aircraft than in other forms of flying. This means there will be a smaller margin for error. However, the danger attached to an activity is often determined as much by the safety consciousness of the approach as by some absolute or measurable risk. In other words, if the safety awareness is tuned to match the potential risk element, no one activity is necessarily more dangerous than another.

At the end of this section there is a list of some 'do's and don'ts' for glider aerobatics, most of which will become apparent to you as you read on. It is not intended to be a check list but may help you to think about some safety points which may not have occurred to you.

A vital part of safety is a clear understanding of the 'Flight Envelope' which you should have in your mind all the time you are flying aerobatics. It is fundamental to aerobatics safety and should be close to every aerobatic pilot's heart.

### Lookout

In gliding, the importance of good lookout is emphasised before anything else. The same applies in aerobatics but even more so. The work load goes up in leaps and bounds when you start learning aerobatics, and as a result your horizon of awareness will often shrink to tiny proportions. At times this tunnel vision effect will reduce your awareness to just the immediate cockpit area. Even experienced pilots are surprised at the extent of this effect and quickly appreciate the value of this awareness phenomenon as a personal tool for assessing their own state of currency. With practice and familiarisation you will eventually develop the ability to keep a good lookout even while performing the most demanding of figures.

The high workload reduces as you make progress, especially if you practise regularly. When workload goes up, lookout goes down... dramatically. So you can see why it is essential to emphasise lookout during training. It is especially useful to include pauses during long or intensive aerobatic sequences in order to thoroughly re-check the whole of the airspace around you. If you practise while other gliding operations are in progress, it is a good idea to choose the quietest area. This is often downwind of your home airfield. Also, inform duty instructors and launch point controllers of your intentions before flying.

### Physiology

Unless you are lucky enough to fly one of the new 'super aerobatic' gliders, such as the

'Fox' or the 'Swift', you are unlikely to be generating the sort of positive or negative **g** loads which can cause loss of consciousness, ie. 'black-out' or 'red-out'. Although susceptibility to these phenomena varies between individuals they will usually occur at sustained g levels in excess of **+8g** or **–4g**. However, you need to be aware that problems can occur at quite modest g loads if sustained for more than a few seconds or when experienced as a reversal between positive and negative values.

When subjected to negative **g** the body's physiology responds in a number of ways. Most noticeable is a considerable reduction in heart rate as our brain quickly notices that less pumping is required to keep it supplied with blood. However, if a sudden reversal from say **–1g** to **+3g** occurs, the brain may take a few seconds to reorganise the physiological change. By this time it may be sufficiently starved of blood to cause dizziness or a momentary 'grey-out' or even 'black-out'. 'Cuban Eights' are particularly good at demonstrating this. The effect can be countered to some extent by holding your breath and pressurising the lower abdomen. (A practice commonly referred to amongst aerobatic pilots by the delightful expression, 'grunting'.) **G** forces also stress internal organs of the body such as the heart, the resultant effect being dependent upon one's age and degree of fitness.

It is important not to underestimate the tiring effect on the body of successive aerobatic sorties and a constant flow of adrenalin. Aerobatic instructors are vulnerable in this respect, and should take regular breaks between batches of 2 or 3 flights. Pilots should also be especially vigilant regarding other factors in their lives, such as stress at work or recuperation from past illness, which can seriously weaken stamina and attentiveness.

## Gusty Conditions

Flying aerobatics in gusty or thermic conditions can be hazardous. In such conditions sudden changes in the velocity of the air through which you are flying can apply loads to the glider in addition to those caused by the figures being flown. If your control inputs are producing loads which are close to the limits of the Flight Envelope then any extra gust loads may well take you outside it. Moderately gusty conditions will produce loads of **0.5g** and very gusty conditions may give **1g** or more. Always make a point of monitoring the g loads caused by gusts while on tow and modify or abort your programme if necessary. (See also the section on Flight Envelopes).

## Daily Inspections

Be particularly vigilant with gliders used regularly for aerobatics. Pay special attention to wing mountings and look for signs of play or overload cracks near control surfaces and airbrake locations. Damage can easily occur if control surfaces are allowed to slam in tail-slides, 'failed' stall turns etc.

Cracks in the wing 'D' box structure orientated at 45° to the spanwise direction should be marked and investigated, as should chordwise cracks in the vicinity of the spar. Both may appear near the root, the airbrake box and the aileron hinges and cut-outs. In composite aircraft, a delamination (swelling of the surface layer) may be noticed by observing the reflected light from the gelcoat surface and indicates that a problem with the underlying structure may exist.

Be sure to vacuum out the cockpit, remove any collected water (did it rain last night?) and ensure the canopy is clean and polished. Never perform aerobatics in a glider you are not familiar with, for example at another club, without checking that someone (preferably yourself) has checked thoroughly for loose items which could jam controls. If necessary remove seat pans etc. to complete the inspection.

**As a final check make sure your parachutes are fully serviced and are not past their inspection date and that you are fully conversant with emergency bale-out procedures.**

## Currency

**M**ost pilots will find that aerobatic flying is demanding on both a practical and financial level. Combine with these factors the relatively small amounts of actual flying time involved and currency becomes a very important issue. Pilots should take a highly responsible approach to assessing their own currency and if in any doubt should always have a check flight with a qualified aerobatic instructor. As a general rule, if you haven't flown aerobatics for more than a month you should regard yourself as non-current. However, your experience level as well as the level of the figures which you propose to fly will have a bearing on this as may other factors. You should also observe local rules which inevitably vary from club to club.

## A Disciplined Approach

**A**erobatics are not a frivolous or daring way of flying but a specific style with clearly defined aims and carefully described criteria. When you are flying aerobatics, be it for practice, competition or display, you should always maintain the highest standards of safety and good airmanship and be careful never to fly outside the limits either of your ability or that of the glider.

Self-discipline is one of the main ingredients of safety. Flying near design limits is safe provided it is done with thoughtful purpose and care. Be especially careful to guard against flying spontaneous manœuvres in a moment of euphoria.

Most pilots will be well aware of the training and discipline required before attempting aerobatic manœuvres, but there will always be those who are tempted to 'experiment' for themselves if they see others doing what look like exciting manœuvres. Imagine . . . you do a low level pull out, beat-up and landing, very expertly flown. A less experienced pilot then attempts to emulate you but comes to grief in the process. You have made a big contribution to his demise.

So for the benefit of others as well as yourself, the message is simple . . .

### *Keep it SAFE, keep it HIGH and be as GENTLE as you can*

*In aerobatics you will be learning to do things with the controls and put the aircraft into attitudes which may be quite alien both to your instincts and to much of what you have learnt in gliding so far.*

*Of course, you should adjust to this new approach gradually and in so doing become more in tune with your aircraft's capabilities as well as your own. But don't lose sight of its limits in the process.*

*Always aim to use only as much speed and g as you need to perform a manœuvre correctly.*

## Emergency Situations

**P**rovided you follow a logical, well defined approach to aerobatic training, progressing through the learnt figures in increasing order of difficulty, it is highly unlikely that you will run into any form of emergency situation. Like any other form of flying, aerobatics will become a fun activity undertaken with a full understanding of what is going on at every stage. If serious problems are encountered, they are likely to include overspeeding/overloading, disorientation and inverted spinning, and it is sensible to consider what you should do in each case.

In the overspeed situation it is **vitally important** that the glider is slowed **by loading the airframe** (pulling **g**) rather than by opening the airbrakes, for reasons which are explained in the following section about Flight Envelopes. However, with excessive speed it is all too easy to overload the airframe beyond the maximum allowable load factor and great care should be taken to avoid this if possible, consistent with pulling as much as one is allowed. Factors of safety used in modern glider design allow for a 50% overload before failure will occur, although permanent structural deformation is possible. In cases of known overload, it is therefore vital that the glider structure is subjected to a detailed scrutiny by a qualified inspector before being flown again.

If you suspect that overload has occurred during flight and provided you have sufficient height (more than 1500 feet) ensure that the glider will respond correctly about all three axes without shedding control surfaces, including the use of airbrakes/spoilers. If all is satisfactory, begin a gentle descent and landing with minimal control inputs. If the glider is obviously damaged, it may be more sensible for you to resort to a parachute descent provided you can do so without the abandoned glider endangering persons or property on the ground. In the case of loss of control, then an emergency bale-out is the only option, and in preparation for this, it is important for you to fully familiarise yourself with bale-out procedures before you fly. Do not waste time, since it can easily take as much as 7 to 10 seconds to achieve a safe descent under parachute, given the difficulties of releasing the glider canopy, releasing lap straps and climbing out of the glider, particularly whilst subjected to significant positive airframe loadings.

Disorientation is most likely to occur during inadvertent spinning which may occur while manoeuvring inverted. Gliders with features which make them spin resistant in erect flight such as washout at the wingtips, will inevitably be more prone to inverted spinning.

The action to be taken in the event of disorientation or inverted spinning is the same, provided that the airspeed is not excessive, namely the application of full and sustained positive spin entry control action until such time as an erect spin or positive spiral dive is recognised. Such control action applied during an inverted spin will result in a positive recovery and entry to an erect spin, provided the glider type is one which will spin with all certainty such as the Puchacz.

Gliders such as the ASK21, which are notoriously difficult to erect spin, will end up in an erect spiral dive which requires prompt recognition and expedient recovery action. This should be effected by rolling then pulling out using elevator to avoid excessive speed build up. Fortunately, in the case of the ASK21, the high $V_{ne}$ of 151 knots together with the drag build up caused by the relatively thick wing helps to reduce these risks. In the event of disorientation at higher speeds, concentrate on levelling the wings with the horizon to stop the spiral dive and then on getting the attitude correct.

Vertical 'Snap Roll' – the world spins around. (*Guy Westgate*)

# Some Basic Guidelines for Glider Aerobatics

## Do's

**Do**  get involved and get trained.

**Do**  get into the habit of monitoring 'g' and speed right from the outset.

**Do**  read the flight manual before flying aerobatics in a new type, and understand the Flight Envelope.

**Do**  regard each manœuvre as an individual entity to be started and completed before setting up for the next.

**Do**  finish all aerobatics (other than simple lines and other exercises) at 1200ft QFE – do it high – especially new manœuvres.

**Do**  'HASSLL' checks before flying aerobatics.

**Do**  tell other pilots of your intentions before take-off.

**Do**  stay current by practising regularly or get check flights, observe currency requirements.

**Do**  regard the spin as the 'standard' recognisable manœuvre to recover from if things go wrong.

**Do**  maintain a disciplined approach to aerobatics at all times.

**Do**  take pride in good airmanship, accuracy and earning aerobatics a good name.

**Do**  prepare aircraft properly before take-off.

**Do**  abort a manœuvre if it is going wrong if you can do so safely (this may not always be possible).

**Do**  take a rest.

**Do**  enjoy it!

## Don'ts

**Don't**  perform aerobatics without a 'g' meter and a serviceable parachute.

**Don't**  perform aerobatics over towns, active airfields, crowds or in controlled airspace.

**Don't**  recover from inverted flight by 'pulling through'.

**Don't**  perform high **g** manœuvres in very thermic or rough conditions.

**Don't**  exceed glider flight limitations (tell people if you do).

**Don't**  try out new manœuvres without prior training/check-out by instructor.

**Don't**  try and hold the controls neutral in an unplanned Tail-Slide, especially the elevator. Hold them hard against the stops from the start to prevent them from slamming against the stops.

**Don't**  forget the importance of lookout when flying aerobatics. Include deliberate pauses in continuous training sequences to re-check.

**Don't**  perform aerobatics at busy flying times.

**Don't**  do manœuvres which frighten you.

**Don't**  fly if you are feeling 'under the weather' or 'hungover'.

**Don't**  show off.

**Don't**  try and imitate more advanced pilots without training.

**Don't**  fly if you are tired, stressed or recovering from illness.

# But do have fun!

ABOVE LEFT & RIGHT:  Different views of the Czech Luňák aerobatic glider. (*Guy Westgate*)
BELOW:  The 15-metre long wing of the Pilatus B4 gives it a slow but graceful roll rate. (*Guy Westgate*)

The German Lö 100 (above) and the Czech Republic Luňák (below) are two vintage pre-war aerobatic gliders, the Lö 100 still being competitive today. (*Mike Woollard*)

ABOVE: 'Unlimited' aerobatic gliders in formation. A Fox leading two Swifts. (*Beat Schück*)
BELOW: A Swift S1 'Unlimited' glider ready to launch. (*Mike Woollard*)

ABOVE: John Gilbert about to fly a fixed undercarriage aerobatic Pilatus B4. (*Mike Woollard*)
BELOW: The Luňák vintage aerobatic glider originally designed to train MiG pilots. (*Mike Woollard*)

# HASSLL Checks

**H** is for Height — Adequate (to finish above 1200ft QFE) bearing in mind distance from the airfield and the lowest point of each figure.

**A** is for Airframe — Limiting speeds ($V_a$ and $V_{ne}$ – note positions/working sectors on ASI), Flight Envelope, flaps, and airbrake positions

**S** is for Straps — Lap strap as tight as possible but without being uncomfortable. Don't forget fifth strap. Re-check as necessary.

**S** is for Security — No loose articles, cameras, glasses, batteries, etc.

**L** is for Location — Not over populated areas, active airfields etc.

**L** is for Lookout — No aircraft below (well banked clearing turns) or flying into your area. At high speeds you can travel a long way in seconds, so try to clear an area forwards as well as below.

Guy Westgate 'poling' the Puchacz. (*Guy Westgate*)

## 2 Flight Envelopes

**W**hile structurally vulnerable on the ground, gliders are really quite strong when subjected to the aerodynamic loads for which they are designed. However, the effect of applied loads varies from glider to glider and with the speed at which the glider flies.

Flying loads which can be applied to a glider are strongly dependent upon airspeed in a way which should be fully appreciated by the aerobatic pilot. Essentially, the ability to apply flight loads increases as the square of the airspeed. To illustrate what this means, if one DOUBLES the speed of flight, then FOUR times the loading can be applied to the glider by the pilot. The implications of this, when $V_a$ and particularly $V_{ne}$ are exceeded, are therefore very serious.

## Pitch Plane Representation

**T**he Flight Envelope is the pictorial way we illustrate the strength of the glider, see Figs 1, 2 & 3.

Each different glider type has its own particular Flight Envelope, eg. Fig 3 which is a graphical representation of the load which a glider can sustain in its most vulnerable direction of control, namely the pitch plane. Loads, as applied by the elevator, are measured perpendicular to both the longitudinal and lateral axes of the glider. The elevator controls the greatest force acting on the glider, the wing resultant force. Changes in this force are the most significant to the airframe.

The load factor 'n' imposed on the airframe is measured as a multiple of gravitational acceleration units, colloquially referred to as '**g**'.

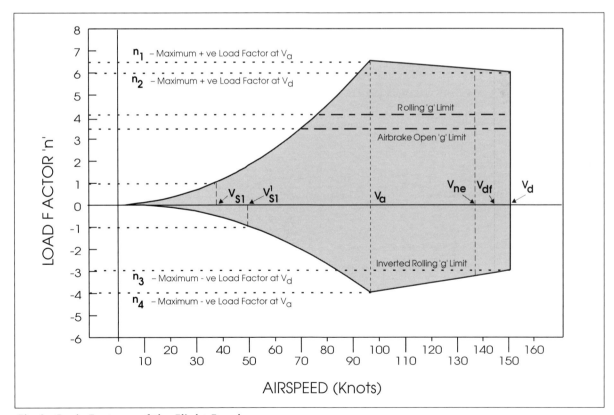

*Fig 1: Basic Features of the Flight Envelope*

An acceleration of **1g** implies that the glider is experiencing its normal all up weight. An acceleration of **2g** means that its weight is effectively doubled. This can be achieved by manœuvring the glider in such a way as to increase the acceleration experienced by the 'mass' of the structure to twice that of gravity. This could be achieved for example in the 'pull-out' from a dive or by 'pulling' the glider around a steep turn, the turn providing an acceleration of **1g** which is additional to the normal **1g** acceleration experienced by the glider in normal level flight. Similarly, accelerations of less than **1g** can be imposed upon the airframe by pushing over to horizontal flight from a steep climb.

Before performing aerobatics in a glider we need a fundamental understanding of its Flight Envelope. Usually, the most difficult task is getting the basic information in the first place as flight manuals often provide only limited information.

Further information should be obtained either from the manufacturers or from other aerobatic pilots. JAR22 is the European design standard for gliders manufactured after   1 April 1980 and provides a valuable insight into the requirements which have had to be met by the glider designers since that time. It is important to realise that gliders designed before that date may not fully meet the strength requirements that are now required by JAR22, so it is important to study the flight manual of the glider you propose to fly.

A very good way of getting to know Flight Envelopes is to practise constructing them, so try drawing the envelope for the type of glider you will be flying. The Appendix gives a step by step guide with reference to Fig 2. If you draw your envelope to the same scale as those in Fig 3 you can then make a direct comparison, but first read the following so you can understand the information provided.

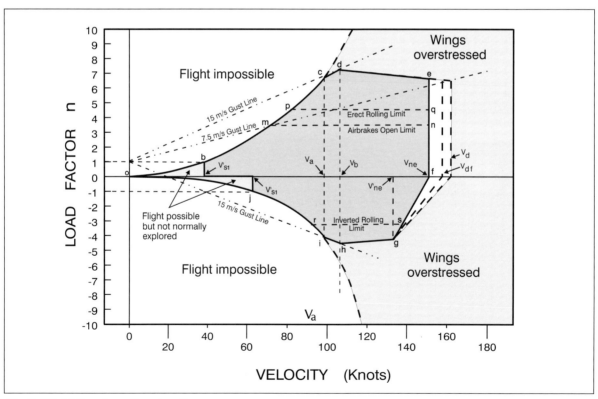

*Fig 2: Flight Envelope Construction*

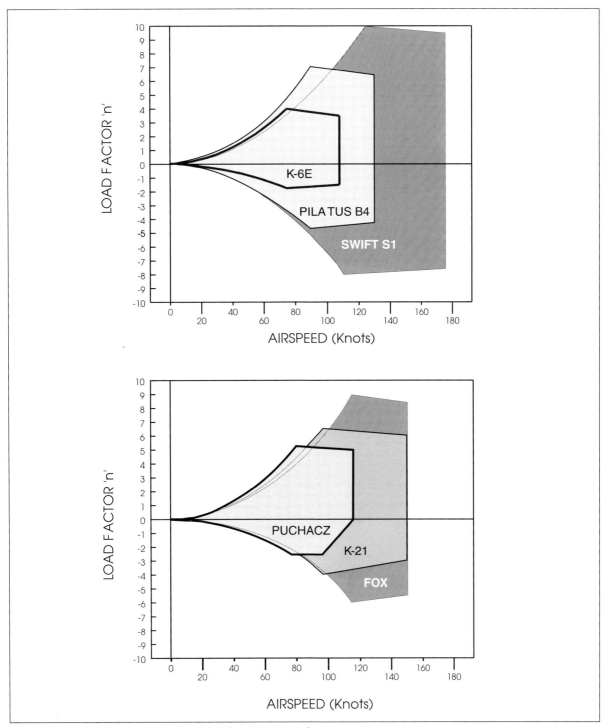

*Fig 3: Flight Envelopes of Different Gliders Compared*

ABOVE: 'Unlimited' aerobatic gliders – the Polish Swift S1 (foreground) and the S. African Celstar behind. (*Guy Westgate*)
BELOW: Flying the Puchacz in momentary knife-edge flight. (*Guy Westgate*)
OPPOSITE: Guy Westgate takes the Puchacz skywards. (*Guy Westgate*)

## Elevator Induced Loads

As already mentioned, the Flight Envelope refers specifically to the elevator, the control with the greatest potential for damaging the airframe. The effect of the other 3 controls (aileron, rudder and airbrakes) is then reflected in relation to the additional constraints which their use imposes.

Referring to **Fig 1** it can be seen that flight loads of **1g** and **-1g** occur at the erect and inverted stalling speeds ($V_{s1}$ and $V'_{s1}$) of the glider. The **maximum manœuvring speed $V_a$** is the next key point. This is the speed beyond which full deflection of the elevator control (only) will cause the wing to generate forces in excess of the maximum designed load. This applies equally in erect or inverted flight although the **load factors ($n_1$ and $n_4$)** are usually of different magnitude because gliders do not use symmetrical wings. $V_a$ and $V'_a$ may also be different.

Between the stall speed $V_{s1}$ and this maximum load condition $V_a$ lies the stall boundary, a curve with its origin at zero. This relates the airspeed to the corresponding load at which the wing will stall with full elevator deflection, thereby alleviating the airframe loads produced. In other words, **up to maximum manœuvring speed, full elevator deflection will not overload the glider**. The wing will stall before a critical load is reached. Above this speed however, overload can certainly occur and judicious use of the elevator is therefore required, reducing to as little as a third of full elevator deflection at the maximum allowable speed $V_{ne}$ of the glider.

JAR22 defines the maximum manœuvring speeds $V_a$ as

$$V_a = V_{s1} \times \sqrt{n_1}$$

where $V_{s1}$ is the erect stall speed and $n_1$ is the maximum erect load factor.

This equation can be used to derive $V_a$ or $V_{s1}$ or $n_1$ in the event that any one value is unknown, for the erect flight conditions. Its application can similarly be used with equivalent values relating to inverted flight, ie $V'_a$ and $V_{s1}$ and $n_4$.

The **maximum design speed $V_d$** will usually be the same but may be different in erect and inverted flight (eg Puchacz). At these speeds, **erect ($n_2$) and inverted ($n_3$) maximum load limits** will normally be lower in value than those occurring at the maximum manœuvring speed $V_a$ and $V'_a$ because the wing inevitably loses some of its bending strength at higher speeds. However, some glider manufacturers simplify the situation by defining $n_1$ and $n_2$ as equal in value and similarly set $n_3$ equal to $n_4$ for inverted flight.

The never exceed speed $V_{ne}$ is established and placarded as 0.9 times the maximum speed demonstrated in flight tests $V_{df}$, which itself must be less than the maximum design speed $V_d$.

JAR22.337 defines the minimum manœuvring load factor limits to which gliders should be designed in either the utility or aerobatic category as shown in Table 1.

However, confirmation of the limits appropriate to type should always be verified by reference to the flight manual in the first instance. The glider may, for example, have been designed only to meet the utility category requirements, the aerobatic load factors therefore not applying.

Gliders are designed to withstand and operate satisfactorily up to their flight limit loads without any permanent structural deformation. The ultimate strength is required to be at least 1.5 times greater, with an ability to resist these loads for at least three seconds before failure occurs.

A further important point is $V_b$ which relates to the rough airspeed limits and the corresponding maximum load factor which is imposed upon the airframe in response to a standard knife edged gust of 15 m/s velocity in the vertical direction. It should not be confused with the maximum manœuvring speed $V_a$ which may be coincident or often lower in value than $V_b$. The position of $V_b$ on the Flight Envelope is determined by the intersection of the 15 m/s gust line with the boundary of the envelope as shown in Fig 2. For completeness it should also be appreciated that the maximum load factor $n_2$ at $V_d$ should be no less than a load imposed by a knife-edge gust of vertical velocity 7.5 m/s. It is a reasonable approximation to take the maximum allowable load factors occurring at $V_a$ and $V_b$ to be the same, ie. $n_1$ in erect flight and $n_4$ in inverted flight.

For a fuller explanation of gust lines the reader should refer to **Frank Irving's** excellent chapter on Flight Envelopes in *New Soaring Pilot* **(Reference 1)**.

| Load Factor | Category | |
|---|---|---|
| | Utility | Aerobatic |
| $n_1$ | + 5.3 | + 7.0 |
| $n_2$ | + 4.0 | + 7.0 |
| $n_3$ | - 1.5 | - 5.0 |
| $n_4$ | - 2.65 | - 5.0 |

*Table 1: Load Factor Limits for Gliders - JAR22.337*

## Factors Moderating the Flight Envelope

Significant additional forces can be imposed on the airframe by the following :

- **Use of rudder to generate yaw forces**
- **Use of aileron to generate roll forces**
- **Use of airbrakes**
- **Vertical up/down draughts**

The effect of these can be seen by referring to the elevator related Flight Envelope, Fig 1, where the reduction each causes to the envelope is shown. Combinations of these effects will reduce the flight limits still further.

Two additional factors which must be taken into account when considering the implications of the Flight Envelope of the glider being flown are:

- **Effects of glider age**
- **Effects of altitude on ASI readings**

### Effect of Rudder

Full rudder and full elevator are generally only used together to perform flick (or snap, as the Americans call them) manoeuvres which, if permitted in the glider in question, will be limited to a maximum airspeed. This should be regarded as the max manoeuvring speed for combined rapid and full deflection of both rudder and elevator controls together (typically **55 knots** on a glider with a $V_a$ of **90 knots**).

---

### WARNING
*Flick manoeuvres impose huge twisting loads on the airframe which severely stress rear fuselage structures, wing and T-tail mountings.*
*They should not be flown in gliders not specifically cleared for such manoeuvres*

---

### Effect of Aileron

A rolling load limit is superimposed on the Flight Envelope as an additional operational limitation when roll control is used. This is a lower figure than the maximum load factor because the wing structure has to provide additional strength in order to withstand the twisting forces caused by the roll control deflection as well as the normal loads. This is illustrated by the roll limit boundary line shown in Fig 1.

JAR22.349 specifies that the positive manoeuvring load factors must not reduce by more than ⅓ when aileron induced loads are imposed on the airframe by full aileron deflection up to $V_a$ and reduced deflection of ⅓ x full deflection at $V_d$ (JAR22.455), ie a load factor $n_1$ of **6** reduces to no less than **4** when full aileron is used at speeds up to $V_a$.

Fortunately, rolling manoeuvres normally occur at low or only moderate airframe loadings so that flight within this reduced Flight Envelope is generally not a problem provided we avoid the use of full ailerons beyond $V_a$. In figures which involve higher speeds and significant elevator and roll controls, more care is clearly required to ensure that they are not used significantly at the same time. Examples of such figures are **Cubans, Cloverleafs** and **Barrel Rolls**.

## Effect of Airbrakes

Contrary to popular belief, use of the airbrakes does cause a significant increase in the loads applied to the glider, requiring a moderation of the Flight Envelope in a similar way to the ailerons, described previously, see Fig 1. The reasons are twofold:

(a) the airbrakes destroy lift over a fairly large inboard section of the wing causing the spanwise wing lift distribution to move outboard. This substantially increases wing bending moments.

(b) the airbrakes also generate drag loads on the wing, a proportion of which become an additional load in the pitch plane direction.

JAR22.345 specifies that the maximum positive load factor limits should reduce to not less than **3.5** with airbrakes fully deployed . . .

> *It is nearly always better to slow a glider by 'pulling g' rather than by opening the airbrakes*

## Effect of Vertical Up/Down Draughts

Loads imposed on the glider airframe by vertical gusts, such as those caused by thermals, detract from the loads which may be imposed by the pilot through the controls. It is clearly inadvisable to pull **4g** in a glider which has a maximum load limit of **5g**, if thermal activity is causing **1g** loads or more at maximum manœuvring speeds. It is therefore best to avoid aerobatics during thermic conditions, leaving them for the smoother air

conditions at the beginning and end of the day.

Fortunately, the loading effect of gusts on the airframe is directly proportional to both the vertical speed of the gust and the glider airspeed. Load excursions of **1g** caused by thermals when flying at 60 knots would translate to only **2g** at an airspeed of 120 knots rather than **4g** as would result from a control input induced load as we noted earlier.

## Effect of Glider Age

New gliders are only flight tested to about 110% of the $V_{ne}$ limit speed and not necessarily to the full design speed $V_d$ which may be of greater value still. As a glider ages its strength will invariably reduce as a result of non-repairable damage (wear and tear) which inevitably occurs throughout its life. A good example of this is the minute loosening of several thousand rivets along the wings of metal two-seater gliders often used for aerobatics, such as the **Blanik**. Pilots should therefore make their own judgement about the age related Flight Envelope shrinkage they consider appropriate for any particular glider they intend to fly.

## Effect of Altitude on ASI Readings

Whilst flying aerobatics we monitor the **g-meter and the airspeed indicator (ASI)** to ensure that we fly within the Flight Envelope of the glider.

As the **ASI** is a **total pressure** measuring device, it is affected by the reduction in air density which occurs with altitude. ASIs will under-read by about **10%** per 5000 feet, such that a $V_{ne}$ of 135 knots becomes 123 knots indicated at 5000 feet, a factor which clearly needs to be taken into account.

This is important for observing airspeed limits (e.g $V_{ne}$ and $V_a$) but it is not a consideration for figure entry speeds where indicated airspeed remains relevant.

## 3 Glider Design

**M**ost gliders are designed primarily for soaring flight rather than aerobatics and they also vary considerably from type to type in ways that are not always obvious. We need to understand how various design features will affect our ability to perform aerobatics for the type in question. Different gliders have quite different aerobatic characteristics so it is not unusual to find a figure which is difficult to perform in one glider but quite easy to perform in another. For example, a glider with a short fuselage and small rudder (eg. **Jantar Standard 2**) will inevitably be difficult to stall turn compared with a glider such as the **Puchacz**. Even the same type will perform differently with different weight pilots in different C of G positions.

Gliders with thick wing sections such as the K21 have the beneficial effect of building drag with speed. This can be very useful in helping to inhibit high speeds as $V_{ne}$ is approached during aerobatic manœuvres. For example, the low $V_{ne}$ of the **Puchacz** makes speed control a particular concern in this otherwise excellent aerobatic two-seater, although the comparatively large wing area makes '**g**-generated drag' very effective in controlling airspeed.

In terms of handling qualities, stick load per '**g**' and aileron design are the defining attributes.

The Lö 100 (above) and Swift S1 (below).

## Table 2: Typical Aerobatic Characteristics of Various Glider Types

| Glider Type | Aerobatic Capability | Aerobatic Suitability | Aero Speed Control | Aerobatic Strength | Spinning Ability | Loops | 60° Stall Turns | 90° Stall Turns | Lazy Eights & Chandelles | Rolling Figures | Inverted Flying | Inverted Spins |
|---|---|---|---|---|---|---|---|---|---|---|---|---|
| K13/K10/K8 | Basic | G | G | Low | OK | Yes | Yes | Yes | Yes | No | No | No |
| K6e | Basic | Poor | Poor | Low | OK | Care | Not Adv | No | Yes | No | No | No |
| K6cr | Basic | G | G | Low | OK | Yes | Yes | Yes | Yes | No | No | No |
| Pirat | Basic | G | G | Mod | Ideal | Yes | Yes | Yes | Yes | No | No | No |
| St'd Jantar | Basic | G | Poor | Mod | Messy | Care | Care | Not Adv | Yes | Half roll | No | No |
| ASW19 | Basic | G | Poor | Low | OK | Care | Yes | Not Adv | Yes | No | No | No |
| Grob G102 | Basic | G | G | Mod | OK | Yes | Yes | Yes | Yes | No | No | No |
| K21 | Int | G | G | Mod | Won't | Yes | Yes | Yes | Yes | Yes | Yes | No |
| Puchacz | Int | G | Mod | Mod | Ideal | Yes | Yes | Yes | Yes | Yes | Yes | No |
| Blanik | Int | G solo | G | Mod | Ideal | Yes | Yes | Yes | Yes | Yes solo | Yes solo | Yes solo |
| Grob Acro II | Int | G | Mod | Mod | Poor | Yes | Yes | Yes | Yes | Yes | Yes | Yes |
| Grob Acro III | Int | G | Mod | Mod | Poor | Yes | Yes | Yes | Yes | Yes | Yes | Not Adv |
| Pilatus B4 | UNL/Int | G | G | High | VG | Yes | Yes | Yes | Yes | Yes | Yes | Yes |
| Lö 100 | UNL | Ideal | VG | High | VG | Yes | Yes | Yes | Yes | Yes | Yes | Yes |
| Swift/Fox | UNL | Ideal | VG | High | VG | Yes | Yes | Yes | Yes | Yes | Yes | Yes |

**Key:** Int = Intermediate • UNL = Unlimited • G = Good • VG = Excellent • Mod = Moderate
• Care = Possible with care • Not Adv = Not Advisable

TOP:  The author's Lö 100 which has won many past championships in the hands of various German pilots. (*Mike Woollard*)
ABOVE:  Peter Mallinson in his Lö 100. (*Mike Woollard*)

TOP:  Aerobatic gliders being prepared at the start of the World Championship. (*Guy Westgate*)
ABOVE:  The Czech Luňák waits for the tow rope. (*Guy Westgate*)

## Table 3: Glider design features and their likely effect on aerobatic characteristics

| Design Feature | Effect |
| --- | --- |
| Highly tapering wing with little or no washout | Easy spin entry – good autorotational behaviour |
| Washout | Good inverted but poor erect spin characteristics |
| No wing dihedral | Reduced stability for light control. Better handling in inverted flight |
| Symmetrical or semi-symmetrical wing | Good inverted flying performance. (Thermalling aerofoils are not ideal for aerobatics) |
| Relatively thick wing | Good drag build-up which helps inhibit high speeds. Also high wing strength which is good for aerobatics |
| Low-set tailplane | Strength in flicks. High tails have high rotational inertia which can twist damage fuselage in flick rolls |
| Powerful rudder moment – large rudder/long fuselage | Greatly assists stall turns and knife-edge flight control |
| High wing incidence relative to fuselage longitudinal axis | Requires inverted flight attitude to be unusally nose high |
| Short wing span | Improves roll and flick rates due to reduced rolling inertia |
| Mid-wing monoplane | Reduced stability for light control response |
| Shoulder or high wing design | May produce roll instability in inverted flight, especially if combined with dihedral |
| Strong construction | Conducive to high 'g' manoeuvres and good speed control |
| Stiff construction (metal, wood or carbon fibre) | High speed flight capability, flutter resistant, crisp control response in roll at high speeds |
| All-flying tailplane | Poor elevator 'stick feel' at speed. All-flying tails are very unsuitable for aerobatics due to low stick load per 'g' |
| Good canopy visibility | Enhances lookout effectiveness. Good for figure shape awareness |
| Strong control stops | Damage prevention if control surfaces allowed to slam in Tail-Slides |
| Airbrakes mounted inboard on wing | High fore and aft wing strength with airbrakes deployed at speed |
| Good speed range with high $V_{ne}$ and $V_a$ | Wide aerobatic repertoire |
| Low drag at speeds up to $V_a$. High drag at high speeds | Good speed control and height management |
| Large main wing area | Good drag producing speed control |
| Large tailplane and elevator area | Good spinning and stalling characteristics |

# 4 Aresti

## What is Aresti?

Aresti was a Colonel in the Spanish Air Force who developed a way of representing aerobatic figures in graphical form based on the performance of the **Bücker Jungmeister** biplane. He categorised different types of figures by identifying just a few fundamental 'building block' manoeuvres such as the loop, the spin, the roll etc. He devised a method of scoring based on multiplying a difficulty factor, the '**K' value**, for each figure by the judge's mark out of ten. In more recent times, with changes in aircraft design, this system was fully revised by a group of aerobatic enthusiasts from around the world and in 1987 a new **Aerobatic Catalogue** was adopted by the FAI Aerobatics Commission (CIVA). This catalogue lists 804 different figures for powered aircraft. In 1990 a new section covering **Glider Aerobatic Figures (Part Two)** was adopted; the 1993 edition listed 556 different figures for gliders.

## Why Aresti?

From all the discussion you may hear during your aerobatic training about 'Aresti' diagrams, judging criteria, programmes etc. you could be forgiven for thinking that aerobatic training is geared toward the serious competition pilot and is therefore not relevant to you. To put your mind at rest, aerobatics is by no means just about competitions and display flying, it is just as much about personal goals and self expression.

The approach described here is aimed at teaching a standard for which there is a well defined and consistent criteria. For this a system is required and Aresti is simply the ideal answer. The symbols are quickly learnt and can convey information more easily than words, particularly to an international audience.

Even at the beginner's level you will soon be flying two or three figures one after the other to form a sequence which you will want to write down in some shorthand form. The following should explain the basics of the 'Aresti' system and enable you to start drawing your own figures at an early stage.

## The Categories of Figures

Fortunately, the whole system can be reduced to just a few simple elements. To start with there are only five basic manoeuvres from which everything else is derived . . .

### • Lines • Turns • Loops • Rolls • Spins

**Figures** are made up from a combination of these **manoeuvres**. There are in fact eight recognised 'Families' of aerobatic figures, and these give us the many hundreds of combinations mentioned above: -

| Family 1 | Lines and Angles |
| --- | --- |
| Family 2 | Turns and Rolling Turns |
| Family 3 | Combinations of Lines |
| Family 5 | Stall Turns |
| Family 6 | Tail-Slides |
| Family 7 | Loops and Eights |
| Family 8 | Combinations of Lines, Angles and Loops |
| Family 9 | Rolls and Spins |

We shall look first at how to draw the figures, then at how to draw programmes . . .

## Drawing the Figures

### The Basic Ingredients

First of all, it is important to appreciate that from the flying point of view all figures start and finish with a horizontal flight path. This is more difficult

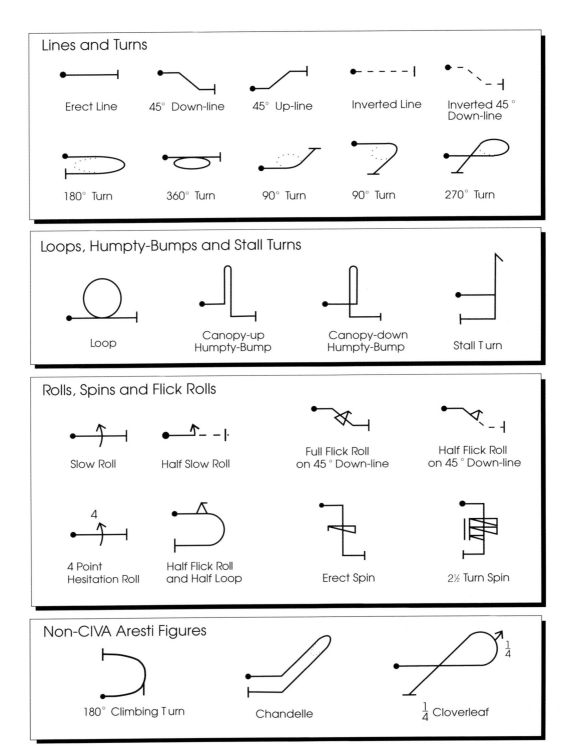

*Fig 4: Sample Aresti Figures*

to achieve in gliders than powered aircraft so when it comes to flying the figures in competitions a five degree down slope is allowed.

Figures are drawn in a very geometric way as if viewed from the side. All changes of direction in the vertical plane from one line to another are drawn, rather unrealistically, as sharp corners. The flight path is drawn as a solid line except in inverted flight where it is a dashed line. The start of a figure is indicated by a solid dot and the end by a vertical line (except where there is a 90° change of direction, then the end line is drawn horizontally).

### Lines and Turns

Only 45° and 90° lines are permitted in the vertical plane and multiples of 90° in the horizontal plane, ie. for turns.

Have a look at the top box of figures in **Fig 4** to see what we have so far. You will notice that when there is a change of heading, as with the 90°, 270° and 180° Turns, the flight path is drawn in a more three dimensional sense in order to give the impression that it is either coming towards you out of the page or going away. A dotted outline of an ellipse is also added to the Turn to further emphasise the type of figure. The direction of the Turn is never specified and can therefore be chosen by the pilot to suit crosswind or positioning considerations.

### Loops, Humpty-Bumps and Stall Turns

Most of you will be familiar with Loops and Stall Turns but you may not know about the **Humpty-Bump**. Briefly, this is rather like a squashed Loop with vertical up and down-lines and a flown (not fall-over) half loop at the top which can be forwards or backwards ('**canopy up**' and '**canopy down**' is the usual terminology, although our American colleagues prefer '**wheels up**' or '**wheels down**'). You will also notice that the exit line of a figure is usually shown lower than the entry if that is what happens in reality, ie. for the Humpty-Bump and the Stall Turn, but not in the case of the Loop.

Now let's look at figures which require some additional notation to be drawn on the line . . .

### Rolls, Spins and Flick Rolls

You will see again in **Fig 4** that for the standard Full Slow Roll an arrow symbol is drawn crossing the main line. In the Half Slow Roll notice how the arrow doesn't cross the line but is drawn from the line and on one side only. This is a standard convention for specifying 'half' and 'full' rotational manœuvres.

Where 'quarter', 'three-quarter' or multiple rotations are to be flown in one figure, the number is always written next to the manœuvre as shown for the **2½ Turn Spin**. The same rule applies to **Spins** and **Flick Rolls**. These are both 'autorotational' manœuvres. A Flick Roll is effectively a more dynamic type of Spin. Its axis of rotation can be along a horizontal line, a sloping line or even a vertical line, though the latter is only for fully aerobatic gliders.

Autorotational figures are depicted by a triangle, again either through or across the flight path line. A right angled triangle depicts a spin, while an equilateral triangle depicts a flick or snap roll. 'Shading-in' the triangle indicates that the spin or flick is initiated with a negative angle of incidence stalling one wing, ie. a negative spin or negative flick as distinct from an 'unshaded' triangle relating to a spin or flick entry initiated with a positive angle of incidence stalling one wing. It is important to realise that positive and negative spins and flicks may be initiated from either erect or inverted flight.

Hesitation rolls are annotated in the same way as standard rolls, but with two numbers included, depicting how many hesitations are to be effected, eg. $\frac{4}{4}$ depicts a four-point hesitation roll, $\frac{8}{8}$ a full eight-point hesitation roll etc.

### Non-CIVA Figures

There are one or two figures which are very useful in basic glider aerobatics which aren't actually recognised in the FAI Aerobatic Catalogue (CIVA) system. These are the **Chandelle, Cloverleaf,** and for training

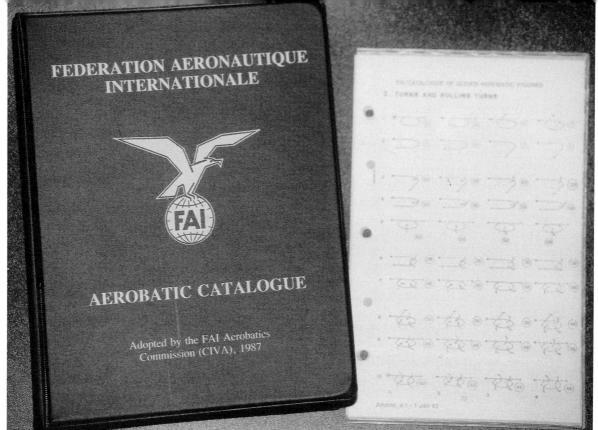

ABOVE:  Pulling the Puchacz up into a Cloverleaf. (*Guy Westgate*)
OPPOSITE ABOVE:  The Aerobatic Catalogue of Aresti figures produced by CIVA. (*Guy Westgate*)
OPPOSITE BELOW:  A reference triangle fitted to a Fox to help pilots fly an accurate line. (*Guy Westgate*)

purposes, the **Climbing Turn**.

The **Chandelle** must be the most undefined of all aerobatic figures and at the 'club' level can be anything from a 150° to a 270° steep turn on a slightly inclined plane (American definition), to a more dramatic hybrid of a near vertical **Stall Turn** and a **Loop**. For the purposes of this book, we define a Chandelle as a figure which begins with level flight, followed by a 45° Up-Line and then a 45° banked turn with the wing reaching a vertical knife-edge at the mid-point of the turn. This is followed by a 45° Down-Line to exit horizontal on a reciprocal heading. It is important to note that the glider is flown all the way round the entire figure.

The **Cloverleaf**, briefly described, involves a combination of looping and rolling such that a Loop which incorporates a 90° change of heading is flown.

The **Climbing Turn** is more an exercise and starts horizontal with a high entry or 'target' speed. The idea is to turn through 180° at a constant angle of bank whilst at the same time smoothly converting speed to height to finish in horizontal flight at a speed only just above the stall.

These will be explained in more detail in the section on *Flying The Figures - Section B*

## Drawing the Programmes

**N**ow we know the basics of drawing the figures we need to know how to string them together to form a sequence or 'Programme'.

The first thing you need is something to draw on. Where would we be without that wonderful little invention the 'Post-it' pad. It has become standard equipment for many aerobatic pilots. Just right for jotting down your programme and sticking it to the instrument panel. You will be able to see from the sample programme, Fig 5, that it is best to start by specifying the wind direction in relation to the drawn programme in the top corner. All competition programmes must start into wind. At more advanced levels it is also a good idea to note other information such as your initials, date, aircraft type, flight

number etc. as you quite often want to refer back to previous flights.

Start in the top left corner. The dot at the beginning of the first figure is always circled and the vertical line at the end of the final figure is always double. Subsequent figures start right next to the end of the previous figure. For a programme of more than a few figures you need to make sure that . . .

- You include figures which produce a suitable change of direction at the appropriate point so you don't disappear from sight on one continuous line.

- The exit speed of one figure is compatible with the entry speed for the next, ie. one figure can actually follow directly from another without the need to make a big speed change.

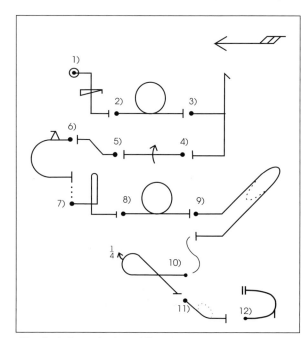

***Fig 5: A Sample Aresti Programme***

OPPOSITE: Aerobatic gliders flying various stages of take-off and landing. (*Mike Woollard*)

Cross box figures are drawn with an entry or exit line at 30° or 60° to the horizontal as illustrated by item 11 of Fig 5.

Where it is difficult to draw a figure without it overlapping with another, the convention is to use a 'squiggly' or dotted line to displace it downwards before continuing to draw the next figure. See aerobatic figures 6 – 7 and 9 – 10 in the sample programme, Fig 5. Always number each figure as shown. This is important when it comes to the 'critiquing' of your flight by a ground observer.

Almost invariably the first figure of a programme will be an 'energy gathering' type needed to launch you into the second figure at a much higher speed. For that reason it is quite common to start with a 45° Down-Line, Spin or Flick Half Roll.

This is by no means the whole story on Aresti but is more than enough to get you through all your initial training and should enable you to draw all the basic figures. Hours of fun can be had on a rainy day devising aerobatic programmes. They are not unlike puzzle games which involve the selection of certain combinations of pieces in order to reach an end point.

And then there's the complicated business of scoring and creating programmes which add up to desired total 'K' values. But we had better leave that for the more advanced training, and a study of the FAI Aerobatic Catalogue (CIVA) (Ref 7).

BELOW: The South African Celstar is a radical 'Unlimited' aerobatic design. (*Guy Westgate*)

# Section B: Flying the Figures

This section covers the following four topics...

Now we come to the moment of truth... how to fly the figures. This is a subject which can easily lead to lengthy description, but remember that no amount of written instruction can be a substitute for actual flying training. However, since there is little literature available on the subject of glider aerobatics this section may be a useful guide to the techniques required for flying the figures.

The figures covered here have been arranged into two groups, **Basic** and **Advanced**. The Basic group covers all those figures which would be found in the 'Sports' class in aerobatic competitions, with the exception of the 'Half Flick Roll and Half Loop'. The Advanced group covers most of the more difficult figures which are included in the BAeA Intermediate level of competition.

| Basic | Advanced |
|---|---|
| • 45° Down-Line | • Tail-Slide |
| • 45° Up-Line | • Inverted Flight |
| • 360° Turn | • Half Slow Roll |
| • Spin | *(from inverted to erect)* |
| • Loop | • Full Slow Roll |
| • Chandelle | • Half Slow Roll |
| • Climbing Turn | *(to inverted)* |
| • Cloverleaf | • Half Cuban Eight |
| • Half Flick Roll and | • 360° Inverted Turn |
| Half Loop | • Pull-Through from |
| • Humpty-Bump | Inverted Flight |
| • Stall Turn | • Reverse Half Cuban |
| | Eight |

## 5 Training Key Points

Before we describe the individual figures, we first need to look at the following aspects of aerobatic flying which will form an important framework for all our training

- **Speed and 'g' Monitoring**
- **Speed Setting and Speed Control**
- **Wing Triangles and Sighting Devices**
- **Visual Cues and Reference Points . . .**
   **'what to look at'**
- **Pause Between Figures**
- **Ground Based Observation**
- **Plan Practice Flights**

### Speed and 'g' Monitoring

You'll need to develop the ability to monitor speed and flight loads so that it becomes a regular and automatic action as soon as possible in your training.

You will soon find that you need to be familiar with critical speeds at many points, both during programmes and during individual figures. You will also need to be acutely aware of $V_{ne}$ and $V_a$. This cannot be over-emphasised, particularly when flying aerobatics in gliders such as the Puchacz which has a relatively low $V_{ne}$ of only 116 knots which it can reach very rapidly.

The same applies to loading. The technique for flying some figures is linked directly to key load factors, so you need to develop the habit of checking your accelerometer. You should also guard carefully against over-loading. It is very easy to become accustomed to high '**g**' and become desensitised. Regular checks on the accelerometer can help to establish one's 'datum'.

TOP: The 2-seat Fox 'Unlimited' aerobatic trainer. (*Mike Woollard*)
ABOVE: The single-seat Swift 'Unlimited' aerobatic gliders are designed and built in Poland. (*Guy Westgate*)

The all-metal Pilatus B4 is an early 'Unlimited' aerobatic glider, outclassed today by the newer Fox, Swift and Celstar designs. (*Mike Woollard*)

When things go wrong, especially at high speeds and high **g** loading, there is a great temptation to 'do nothing' in the hope that somehow it will all sort itself out. This is a dangerous assumption and can result in over-speeding and over-stressing. These can be averted quite easily with the correct control inputs . . .

> ### Guard against INACTIVITY if things go wrong.
>
> ### If speed starts to build DON'T RELAX Push, Pull or Roll as necessary and MAINTAIN CONTROL

## Speed Settings

In aerobatics, speed accuracy takes on a whole new meaning. It is one of the key skills which the beginner needs to cultivate in order to fly accurate figures. You may think your speed control is already good. This may well be true in steady flight or even when asked to change attitude, but in aerobatics you will need to be able to do much more. For example, you may have to recover from a vertical dive. ie. immediately after spinning or rolling, in a pull-out which you know will leave you with exactly 100 knots. You will be setting and re-setting speeds over and over again throughout a programme with very little time for adjustment. As airspeed changes you will need to learn to compensate and allow for trim changes which occur, as well as the lag in the indicated airspeeds inherent in the airspeed indicator.

> *Aim for precision and discipline in speed setting right from the outset*

## Wing Triangles and Sighting Devices

You may already have seen fluorescent coloured triangular wire frames attached to the wingtips of some aerobatic gliders and wondered what these 'coat-hanger'-like devices were for. They enable the pilot to accurately compare the angle of the fuselage with the horizon and to set accurate 45° and vertical lines.

Although it is possible to do this by looking along the wing, this cannot be as accurate. The problem is that the 'rigging angle', or 'angle of incidence' at which the wing is attached to the fuselage (see Fig 23), minus the somewhat smaller angle of 'washout' of the tip, means that the 'tip chord' may not be aligned with the fuselage centre line. Setting the tip chord at right angles to the horizon, eg. in order to give you a vertical up-line, may mean that the fuselage centre line will be a few degrees short of the vertical. Couple this with only a few degrees of pilot inaccuracy and a substantial error can occur, and the figure will not look correct to a ground observer. Worse still, on some critical figures such as a vertical Stall Turn, an unpleasant Tail-Slide or fall over could occur.

Other sighting devices commonly used include lines drawn on the canopy sides using a chinagraph pencil, and small tufts of wool to indicate airflow changes such as high angles of attack and rearward motion in a Tail-Slide.

## Visual Cues and Reference Points:

### or 'What to look at'

Accuracy is one of the fundamental requirements of aerobatics. Knowing where to look for the best cues during a figure is one of the keys to accurate flying.

In all figures we need to judge and maintain attitudes, lines and angles continuously. Most pilots already have a keen awareness of the horizon over the nose of the glider, but we need to practise additional observation skills. We shall want to be able to detect small changes in angles of bank and pitch not only during wings level flight but at other times during a figure. In the initial stages of practising a new figure it can often help to verbalise visual cues and consciously think about a correction so that with repetition and practice it becomes automatic; eg.

looking out at the horizon to determine whether your wings are level at the top of a loop.

By tracing through a figure we can establish exactly what we want the glider to be doing at each stage. We can then organise our visual cues (including instruments) to achieve an overall lookout which gives us all the information we need, when we need it.

Some aspects of accuracy can be gauged from the cockpit, although cross and head-wind effects can make this difficult at times. However, many accuracy points such as the 'roundness' of a Loop can only be judged by a ground observer. In order to check accuracy from the cockpit, reference points are needed. We therefore need to practise with two types: **Ground Lines** and **Point References**.

The **Ground Line** can be any straight line feature which is very obvious from the air. It might simply be a road, canal, runway or railway line, but could also be a vegetation change line or the centre line of an elongated but perhaps irregular feature such as a wood. It is also important to have some reference point on an extension to the ground line for when the glider is directly overhead and the pilot can no longer see the ground line itself. Heading accuracy will be required in all figures and is extremely difficult without a recognisable **ground line** and associated reference points.

**Point references** are required in many different locations. They may be on the horizon, vertically below you, 45° ahead, 45° above etc. Some are used repeatedly while others apply at one moment only. Distant references don't have to be point objects such as cooling towers or grain silos. Often more useful are large objects such as towns, woods, hedgerows, yellow rape fields and even clouds. Whatever they are you should get used to looking for them and using them throughout an aerobatic sequence.

Unfortunately there is a small penalty to pay which may compromise this process at times; moving the head while experiencing anything other than **1g** will result in misleading sensations of motion, which can even lead to nausea.

Unfortunately, without moving the head we are denied our most useful information so we must train ourselves to rely on our eyes and not our balance sensations. Pilots with experience of instrument flying will be familiar with this phenomenon.

*Example*

Now let's put all these points together in an example and see 'what to look at' during the simple transition from straight and level flight to a 45° Down-Line. First, let's think what we need to do . . .

| A | Keep wings level and speed constant in the initial horizontal section |
|---|---|
| B | Keep wings level during pitching down |
| C | Pitch smoothly and stop cleanly at 45° nose down |
| D | Hold a straight 45° Down-Line, wings level |

**For A** we can keep the wings level by monitoring the horizon over the nose. If in doubt (and we have time at this stage) we can glance at each wingtip in turn for a more accurate assessment. A constant speed can be ensured by maintaining a constant attitude. Here again the horizon is the primary source of information.

**For B** as we start to pitch, the initial angle we achieve is not important, so there is no need to look to the wingtip yet. The most useful cue is still the horizon which enables us to keep the wings level.

**For C** we can make a qualitative judgement of pitching rate, in order to keep the pitching smooth, by watching the horizon move up the canopy. Just before we reach 45° (any sooner will waste valuable observation time) glance down the wing and stop the rotation crisply at 45°. It will be a new skill to judge the angle of the wingtip against the horizon.

ABOVE: Pilatus B4 going vertical with wings aligned to the active runway at Lasham. (*Terry Joint*)
OPPOSITE ABOVE: Preparing the 2-seat Fox for flight. (*Peter Mallinson*)
OPPOSITE BELOW: The original L13 Blanik, which was for many years an eminent 2-seat trainer for aerobatics. (*Pavel Lukes*)

**For D** in order to maintain the 45° line we must instantly find a reference or aiming point on the ground directly ahead in the flight line and actively fly the glider to keep this point stationary on the canopy. This will help us overcome the tendency for the nose of the glider to rise as speed builds in the dive. The horizon will be in our upper periphery and will enable us to keep the wings level. As the speed increases the instruments must be included in a fast scan between ASI and our reference point in order to time the pull-out.

With this approach, ie. by carefully establishing exactly how we plan to judge and monitor each section of a figure, we can work out an order for observing the necessary visual cues.

## Pause Between Figures

Although an aerobatic sequence may appear to be flown in a continuous flowing way, in practice each figure is a discrete entity with a beginning, a middle and an end. For both safety and consistency of execution, successive figures in a sequence should be separated by a pause in horizontal flight which is discernible from the ground. It may only be a second or two but is most important. If figures are run together there is a real danger of both **g** and speed build-up as it is no longer possible to pause in a more stabilised attitude to check and adjust the entry conditions ready for the next figure.

This pause also provides a chance to glance at the Aresti programme card to check which figure comes next and the entry speed requirement. It is also an excellent moment to check look-out and positioning.

As you gain experience these pauses will naturally shorten, but are never eliminated, even though they may appear to be to the uninitiated.

## Ground Based Critique

Aerobatics are performed very much with the ground observer in mind, whether spectator or judge. A figure is judged to be flown correctly by its appearance from the ground rather than because the pilot felt he flew it correctly. Ideally, have someone observe your flight and make notes, preferably using a portable tape recorder. You can then discuss them together afterwards.

In observing the shape of figures flown, the ground observer will be concerned with either the orientation of the fuselage, often referred to as the **zero lift axis (ZLA)** or the passage of the centre of gravity of the glider, known as the **Centre of Gravity Track (CGT)**. Different parts of different figures require attention to one of these aspects. For example, the up and down lines of a Stall Turn or Humpty-Bump are judged ZLA where the fuselage is required to be exactly vertical. A looping manoeuvre, however, is judged CGT, where the C of G of the glider is required to describe a circle, but the attitude of the fuselage may be adjusted to correct the CGT for the effects of wind. Similarly, a 45° Up-Line or Down-Line is judged ZLA with CGT corners.

## Plan Practice Flights

It is a good idea always to plan your flight. Try not to take off only with a general idea about what you intend to do, except perhaps if you plan to work specifically on one or two figures. Always draw a programme and try to stick to it. In case it goes wrong for any reason, have in mind whether you intend to start again, break and continue as you would in a competition, or some other plan, but do have one. This point is especially relevant when training for competitions.

Your time in the air is very precious. The more you can plan and prepare on the ground the more useful will be your time in the air and the more you will learn from your practice.

As you progress and fly aerobatics in a variety of different gliders, it is useful to keep a small notebook of load and speed limits and ideal target entry speeds for each glider type, to help with this planning process.

# 6 The Basic Figures

One of the problems inherent in describing how to fly aerobatic figures in any detail is the variation in technique required between one glider type and another. Neither are the differences small. A set of instructions for one type cannot necessarily be used for another, especially when it comes to speeds. However, there are many points which will apply to all gliders.

The following chapter gives only the general technique required to fly the figures, starting with the basics and taking you through to the more advanced figures. The speeds given are therefore only indicative of those likely to be required and are, in the main, based on experiences with the ASK21, the Grob Acro and the Puchacz.

The notes for each figure start with a brief description of how it should look to an observer (it is handy to know what you are trying to do before you do it). This is followed by a list of some of the most common faults, again as they would appear to a ground observer. Finally, there is a detailed description of the technique required to fly each figure correctly.

For each figure it is necessary to ensure that you are correctly lined up with the ground line and heading in the right direction towards a selected reference point in the distance. Your wings should be level with no yaw present and you should have just completed the short horizontal line at the start of the figure and established the appropriate target entry speed for the figure you are about to perform.

The 'target speed' is the speed at which you initiate control inputs for the figure. It is preferable that the short 'horizontal' line at the start of a figure should be at a near constant speed. With a small nose down attitude of 5° (the maximum permitted in competitions) this will usually be possible. However, with some figures this may be more difficult; the entry speed at the beginning of this line, ie. the beginning of the figure, may not be the same as the target speed.

Exit speeds from most figures can be varied and will usually be determined by the target speed required for the next figure.

## The 45° Down-Line

A short horizontal line should be followed by a pitch transition to a 45° Down-Line held steady for a moment before pitching back to another straight horizontal line. The radii of both the pitching segments should be the same. The 45° line is judged on fuselage angle or ZLA and should not be wind corrected.

**Common faults** are: not establishing a full 45° Down-Line, not keeping wings level while pitching to the down-line, allowing the nose gradually to rise during the down-line and generally not keeping the line straight.

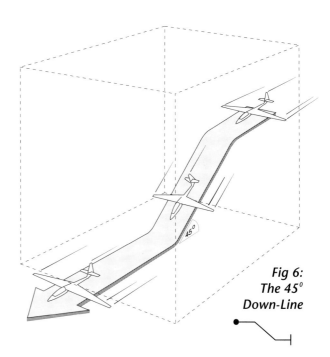

*Fig 6: The 45° Down-Line*

**Target entry speed** should be very slow, ideally not more than about five knots above the stall. The slow start gives plenty of time in the down-line to monitor your reference point and other visual cues before having to level out. It will also ensure a good length to the down-line which otherwise can appear surprisingly short to a ground observer.

A positive pitch down manoeuvre should be initiated without generating too much negative **g**. Just before you reach 45°, glance briefly at the wingtip to check the angle against the horizon so you can stop the pitching accurately at 45°. Immediately look straight ahead and select the point on the ground which is directly in line with your flight path. Keeping your wings level by reference to the horizon, use this forward reference point to maintain a constant attitude in the same way as you use the horizon in horizontal flight. This will ensure a straight down-line and overcome a common tendency to shallow out the dive as the speed builds and the trim changes.

As soon as possible monitor your ASI and when the needle reaches a speed 5–10 knots (depending on type) less than the desired exit speed (to suit the next figure) pitch up to the horizontal using no more than **3g**. As you rotate and regain level flight be careful to keep the nose below the horizon, resisting the temptation to pull up. This is something nearly all beginners find difficult because of the natural reaction to reduce high speeds by climbing. Monitor your ASI to ensure that your speed does not drop below the desired exit speed and check again that your wings are level.

Prior to your first attempt it is valuable to get your instructor to show you how to establish the shallow 5° energy maintaining exit line so that you can get used to the attitude required.

## The 45° Up-Line

This should look like a mirror image of the 45° Down-Line. It is not wind-corrected and is judged on the basis of fuselage angle or ZLA relative to the horizon.

**Target entry speed** should be anything from 90–110 knots if possible, but in practice it will be whatever the previous figure allows. A higher speed will have the advantage of a longer up-line which in a competition can be useful for judging

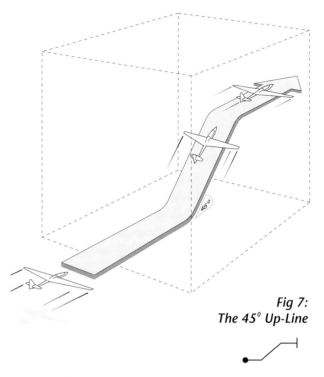

**Fig 7:**
**The 45° Up-Line**

purposes. Pitch the nose up smartly with not less than **2g** to a 45° Up-Line and then maintain a straight flight path by picking a reference point in the sky if there is one. While you still have enough speed push over smartly to the horizontal.

**A common fault** with the 45° Up-Line is leaving the push-over into the final straight and level section too late. Use the ASI as a guide and push over at an indicated speed of 15–20 knots above the desired speed for the horizontal line.

# WARNING
*Gliders with pronounced spin characteristics can be very susceptible to spinning, particularly at reduced g levels, in the push-over from the '45° Up-Line', so take care with this figure particularly at lower altitudes.*

52

## The 360° Turn

You may be surprised to learn that this is indeed an aerobatic figure, but when you try and fly it accurately you will discover that it is not quite as easy as it looks. It should consist of a horizontal line followed by a rapid roll to a 60° banked turn which should be accurately maintained. A constant radius well co-ordinated circle should be flown with a roll out on the original heading.

**Common faults** are: insufficient and varying angle of bank and pitch, and flying the whole figure too slowly.

**Target entry speed** is generally not less than 60 knots. Roll with at least ¼ control deflection to an angle of bank of 60° without changing heading. This may require a little opposite rudder before the turn commences. Then turn and if possible maintain the bank angle and speed as carefully as you can. When you have turned through about 315° look round for your ground reference line and roll out on the original heading, wings level, in horizontal flight.

There are essentially three parts to the turn. Rolling in – turning – rolling out. Or, put another way, roll without turning – turn without rolling – roll out without turning again.

Similar criteria apply to all other Turns regardless of heading change.

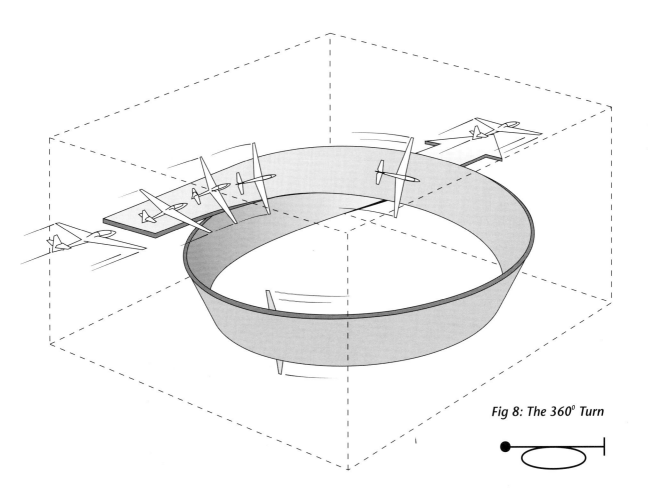

*Fig 8: The 360° Turn*

## The Spin

The Spin at least may seem like familiar territory to you, although like many pilots you may regard spinning exercises as something to be avoided or viewed with apprehension. Even if you are reasonably confident about spinning you may be surprised to discover just how much more confidence you will have when you become acquainted with spinning in its aerobatic form with a controlled exit on to a heading.

Aerobatics training should transform any apprehension you might have about spinning into confidence and enthusiasm for this really fascinating and challenging figure.

From level flight the spin entry should give the impression that the glider drops directly into a steady spin with no discernible pitch up of the nose or hesitation or other interruption to the flight path. The spinning should be symmetrical and uniform with a crisp stop in a vertical nose down attitude at recovery. A short vertical down-line is then held, followed by a high speed horizontal line on the defined heading.

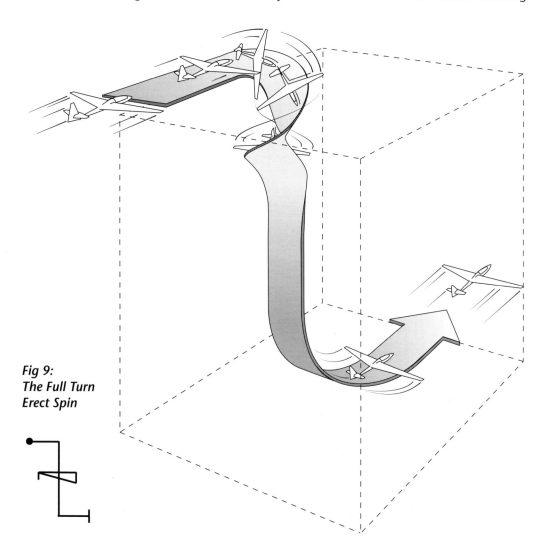

*Fig 9:*
*The Full Turn*
*Erect Spin*

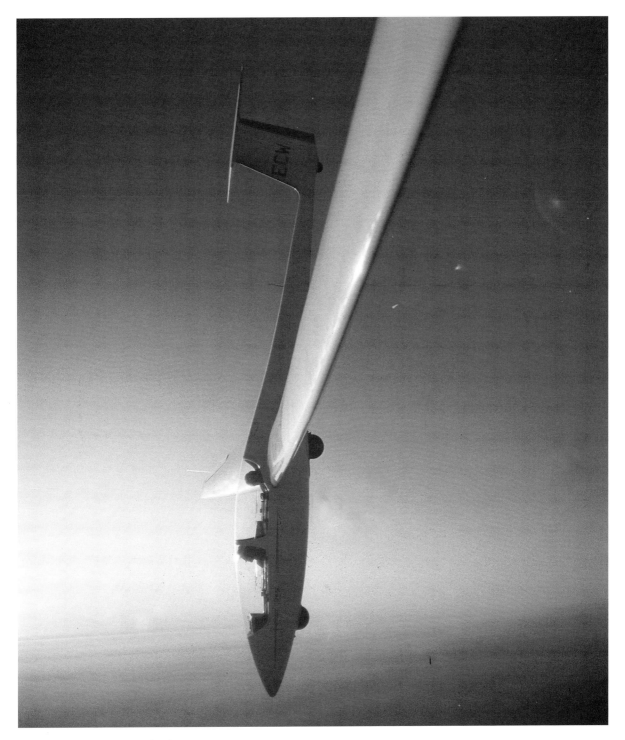

Time to go down. (*Tony Hutchins*)

ABOVE:  The Czech Luňák vintage aerobatic glider in flight.
(*Paul Mellor Photography*)
OPPOSITE:  The Lö 100 in a traditional aerobatic sunburst
colour scheme. (*Guy Westgate*)

The subject of 'aileron-aided spin entry' is rather a mine-field. Whether 'in-spin', 'out-spin' or 'neutral aileron' should be used and in what quantity and when will be dictated by a combination of design features and C of G positions. Generally, out-spin aileron has the effect of flattening the spin and is therefore beneficial with more forward C of G positions (ie. heavy pilot combinations). In-spin aileron usually steepens and stabilises the spin which can promote premature recovery particularly with a heavy crew. Ideally, spins should be carried out with neutral aileron.

**Common faults** are: pitching up at the start into a more dynamic entry; trying to enter too fast or not properly stalled (ie. stick not fully back) resulting in a spiral dive rather than a spin; recovery off-line; non-vertical exit line; not using full rudder at recovery; using aileron at recovery and recovery to a climbing attitude as in standard club training practice.

It is important to use and maintain a consistent entry technique so that the rates of spin, yaw and roll are always the same. This will ensure a consistently accurate exit on the desired heading using the same 'lead angle'.

### Entering the Spin

**Target speed** is typically 2 to 5 knots above the stall. Maintain a true horizontal attitude so that your speed reduces and at 2 to 5 knots above the stall yaw the glider fully by steady and full application of the rudder (hence the extra few knots which ensure sufficient rudder authority and a good rate of yaw). At the same time, but slowly at first, bring the stick back along the centre of the box enough to stop the nose from dropping but without raising it. The stick should reach the fully back position at the same moment as the rudder reaches full deflection. The rearward stick movement will be progressively more rapid so that the final movement will be quite abrupt. At this point on more spin resistant gliders it may also be beneficial to apply momentary in-spin aileron to assist the start of autorotation.

The glider should start to autorotate straight away at this point without any appreciable hesitation or pitching up of the nose.

### Maintaining the Spin

Hold the stick firmly against the back-stop in the central position. Maintain full rudder deflection and allow the aircraft to rotate freely. Notice your orientation both with the ground line and with the horizon. The attitude will be quite nose down. At each half rotation count out loud, 'Half… one… one and a half' etc. This will help you avoid becoming disorientated or losing track of when to recover. This is a very common problem when spinning, even at advanced levels. (In the earlier stages of training it may aid work-load problems to count only full turns.)

### Recovery from the Spin

It takes quite a time from the moment you initiate recovery action for most two-seaters to stop spinning. You therefore need to start taking action well in advance, so at least 90°, if not 120°, before the recovery heading take the standard initial recovery action: apply full opposite rudder and then push the stick forward.

When the spinning has stopped, make corrections if necessary to line up with the ground line, but do not pull back on the stick immediately to pull out of the dive as you normally would. In fact, in order to achieve the vertical exit line you must quickly pick a ground reference point vertically below you and, as the spinning stops, push the stick forwards to hold the nose on this point, but for only a moment. This is particularly important in more 'slippery' gliders such as the Puchacz or $V_{ne}$ will approach very quickly. For this reason it is better to set your down-line angle by picking a reference point directly below you than by attempting to check your wingtip or triangle against the horizon as you would in a 45° Down-Line. (In the early stages of training we will not necessarily be aiming for a fully vertical exit.) Pull out of the dive well before $V_{ne}$, monitoring your speed all the time and keeping the wings level. Keep checking your alignment and finish on a horizontal line at the desired entry speed for the next figure.

To start with you will almost certainly have difficulty judging how long the recovery takes (ie. how many degrees of rotation) to stop the glider spinning from the moment you initiate recovery. This will vary from type to type and with different C of G positions.

When you have established this you will know just how much 'lead' to give. The angle is typically 90–120°. You then need to be precise about initiating the recovery. As you become more accomplished at this you may find it helpful to work out just how much you can relax the full up-elevator and into-spin rudder while you are still spinning without provoking recovery. You will then be able to hold the glider in the spin but on the verge of recovery. This gives more precise control over the timing.

Again, as you become more experienced you may also find that recovery can be effected simply by centralising the controls. This will work for most types provided it is done fairly sharply.

The above techniques are, however, further complicated when spin exits are required at quarter or half turn points where the different dynamics of the spin may require more or less lead than in the one turn case.

## The Loop

Probably because of its relative simplicity this is one of the most popular of all aerobatic figures, especially with spectators who are not specialists. Most pilots who want to learn aerobatics have already done a fair number of Loops. Equally it is a figure which is difficult to perform well with the following key features properly stressed.

Quite simply a Loop should be a horizontal line followed by a constant radius circle in the vertical plane with a horizontal exit line. Appreciable wind strengths can make it quite difficult to maintain the circular shape. The roundness is judged by the path of the glider's C of G (or CGT) so adjustments must be made for wind effects.

**Common faults** are: not keeping wings level, losing too much speed at the top and either falling over or dropping a wing, tightening the circle after the top and exiting off-line. A common mistake in strong winds (or a common problem if there is no choice in the matter) is to fly a Loop down-wind. This has the effect of drawing out the Loop so much that the radius at the top will appear very small and in extreme cases, despite using the correct technique, can even look 'thorn'-shaped thus . . .

**Wind Direction**

*Fig 10: A 'Thorn' Shaped Loop*

It is important to start a Loop with the wings absolutely level and with no yaw. This should be checked again at five points during the Loop:

1. at the start
2. whilst pitching up
3. at the top
4. on the way down
5. after the exit

ABOVE and BELOW: Flying an ASK21 around a Loop. (*Guy Westgate*)

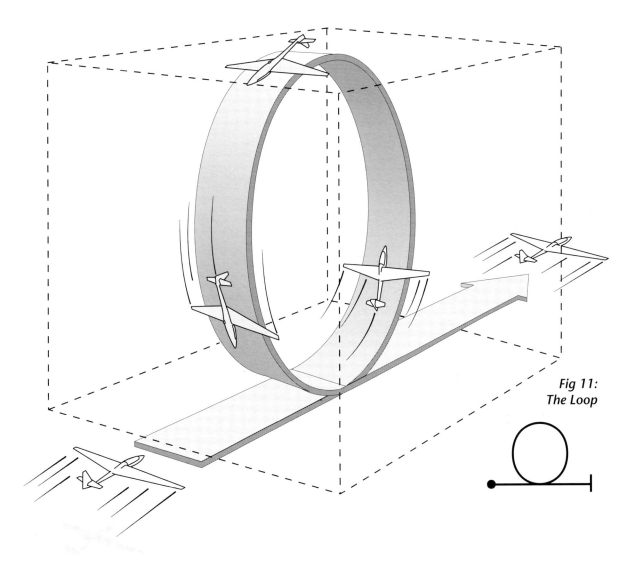

*Fig 11:*
*The Loop*

**Target Speed** is usually a minimum of 2½ times stalling speed. Pull back to achieve a minimum of **3g** in the first quarter. Just as you start to pull back it is important to check the horizon and the yaw string to ensure that you are still correctly lined up with level wings. This must be done in the first 10° or so before the ground ahead disappears below the nose and several seconds worth of valuable visual information are gone for good. In order to continue an accurate pull-up after this point it can be surprisingly helpful to project and then follow an imaginary vertical line from the nose upwards to represent your intended flight path.

In the second quarter, as speed decays and the effectiveness of the elevator reduces, progressively ease back on the stick to maintain a constant radius (**g** and stick load will be steadily reducing). Unfortunately, you cannot view the radius you are flying. This can only be done by an observer on the ground, so you may need to relate this to the rate of pitching which you can see.

This is a good example of the valuable role a ground observer can play. However, a smooth pitching rate alone is a good starting point for achieving a circular Loop.

As you approach the inverted, look well back over your head in order to locate the horizon again as soon as it comes into view. At the same time check alignments and correct as necessary. At this point, **g** should not fall below zero and ideally should remain above +¼.

When you reach the inverted position at the top of the Loop relax the back pressure slightly, for a moment only, to reduce the rate of rotation and keep the radius constant with minimum speed. This will delay the dropping of the nose which will otherwise tend to fall too rapidly into the second half of the Loop, tightening the circle as it does so. Pressure should then be quickly but steadily re-applied and the stick moved slowly aft again in order to maintain the shape of the third quarter. (NB: the back-pressure must not be relaxed too much at the top, or for more than a moment, otherwise speed will start to build rapidly in an inverted dive.)

By this time you should be making any adjustments needed to align with the ground line. As you progress into the fourth quarter, speed will be building fast. Monitor speed closely and relax back-pressure steadily as the elevator becomes more effective in order (a) to achieve the target entry speed for the following figure and (b) to avoid an unnecessarily harsh pull-out and tightening of the Loop. When correctly flown the **g** changes during a Loop should be smooth and flowing.

A key feature of the Loop is the achievement of a constant radius throughout the figure to give it a circular shape. This involves applying the correct amount of elevator deflection as the airspeed changes. Essentially the pitch rate used needs to be proportional to airspeed. High airspeed – high pitch rate. Low airspeed – low pitch rate. You will know you have finally got it right on the day that you feel a little 'bump' on recovery as you fly through the wingtip vortices which you created at the start of the figure.

## The Chandelle

This is another popular 'club', but non-FAI, figure. But you will rarely find two people who have the same ideas about what it should be. In America it is referred to as 'half a Lazy Eight' as noted by Neil Williams, in his book *Aerobatics*, (Ref. 5). An American 'Chandelle' is what we in the UK used to call a 'Climbing Turn'. It is often suggested that this figure would be more appropriately referred to as a 'Wing-over' as it is more in line with this figure as it is defined in other countries.

For the purpose of standardisation we describe the Chandelle as a horizontal line followed by a 45° up-line. At the top there is a 180° constant radius turn at a 45° angle of bank. The roll out of this turn should be into a 45° down-line parallel with the up-line. (The up- and down-lines need only be established; they are not required to be held. However, if they are held then they must be of equal length.) The down-line is then followed by the final horizontal line on a reciprocal heading to the entry line. At the highest point of the turn the wings should be pointing vertically up and down in the knife-edge attitude.

**Common faults** are: insufficient energy to complete the turn-round as a fully flown element. This is often due to a slow entry speed, taking too long to rotate into the up-line, holding the up-line too long or taking too long over the turn-round. All these errors will make keeping alignments almost impossible.

**Target Speed**: this figure may be flown successfully from a range of target speed from 70–100 knots. However, at the slower speeds the energy available for the up-line may be insufficient for it to be held for more than an instant. Pitch the nose up smartly with not less than 2½**g** to a 45° up-line. Hold this line straight using a reference point in the sky if there is one, for no more than a second. This will leave as much speed as possible for the next stage. Roll at maximum rate to 45°, stop rolling and fly a constant radius and constant bank 180° turn. Roll out at maximum rate again to a 45° down-line parallel with your original up-line. Hold this line again only momentarily then pull back smartly to horizontal flight at your target exit speed.

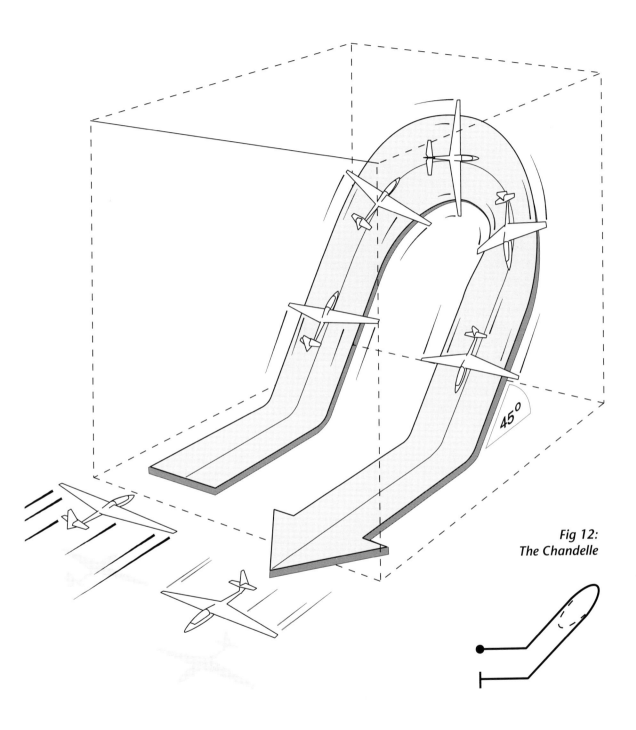

*Fig 12:*
*The Chandelle*

The Puchacz flies the 45° up-line of the Chandelle. (*Guy Westgate*)

## The Climbing Turn

Like the Chandelle, this figure is not in the FAI Catalogue, but it has great value as a training exercise. For an apparently simple figure it requires considerable co-ordination, judgement and timing. As such it can be a profitable way of using up excess speed at the end of a training programme or a practice sequence and can be safely flown below the 1200ft minimum height advisable for the more demanding figures.

The aim, as mentioned in an earlier section, is to turn through 180° at a constant angle of bank and radius whilst at the same time climbing, to finish horizontal at a speed just above the stall on a reciprocal heading. This is a difficult exercise as it means setting up a climbing turn which will give the correct rate of energy loss, leaving you at normal flying speed at the end.

**Common faults** are: running out of energy, usually as a result of raising the nose too high in the turn leaving insufficient speed to roll back to horizontal; not maintaining a constant attitude throughout the turn; allowing the angle of bank to increase to very steep angles causing nose drop and speed increase.

**Target Speed** may be 70–90 knots. Roll fast, at the same time keeping the nose on a reference point ahead (ie. rolling without turning) to a 60° angle of bank. The moment this angle has been achieved, feed in up elevator and pull back into a 180° turn at a 60° angle of bank.

Once the angle of bank has been established on the original heading the primary source of the turning element is the elevator. In order to incorporate the right amount of speed loss in the turn you will need to raise the nose higher than normal to about 15–20° above the horizon where it will stay for the duration of the turn, provided the angle of bank is held constant. After about 90° of the turn, look round until you can see the ground line and monitor your alignment constantly for the remainder of the turn to ensure that you roll out and finish on an accurate reciprocal heading.

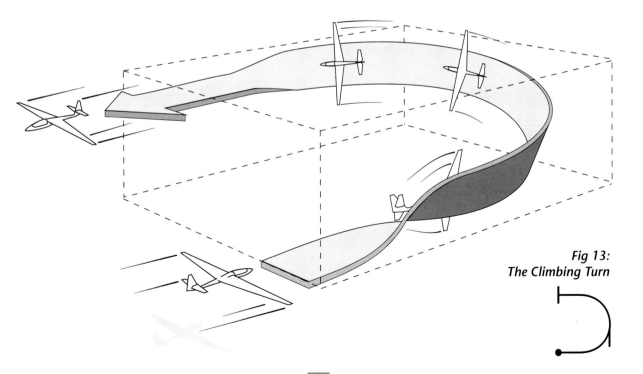

*Fig 13:*
*The Climbing Turn*

## The Quarter Cloverleaf

The Cloverleaf is essentially a combination of looping and rolling. It is considered a basic figure, but because of the rolling element it should be practised with some caution, ideally once rolling has been mastered. Again this is a non-FAI Catalogue figure.

The glider should pitch up from horizontal flight as for a Loop, but it should roll at the same time during the second quarter so as to change heading by 90° as the glider reaches the inverted. It should then continue to complete the loop with no further rolling to exit on a horizontal line at right angles to the entry line. A sequence of four identical ¼ Cloverleafs will produce the Full Cloverleaf. Each will give a

heading change of 90° so that the exit is on the same heading as the entry line. However, this is not recommended until you have mastered the ¼ Cloverleaf. Since the shape of this figure is judged on the glider's virtual track or CGT, wind correction will be required as necessary.

**Common faults** are: failing to combine the rolling with the looping element in the correct proportions, resulting in an unevenly shaped figure and an exit off line, and initiating the roll too early, resulting in excessive speed once inverted, or even a failure to achieve a wings level inverted attitude.

**Target Speed** is slightly more (5–10 knots) than for a straight Loop because of the extra energy needed for the rolling action. Entry is as for the Loop. Pitch the nose up and continue rotating,

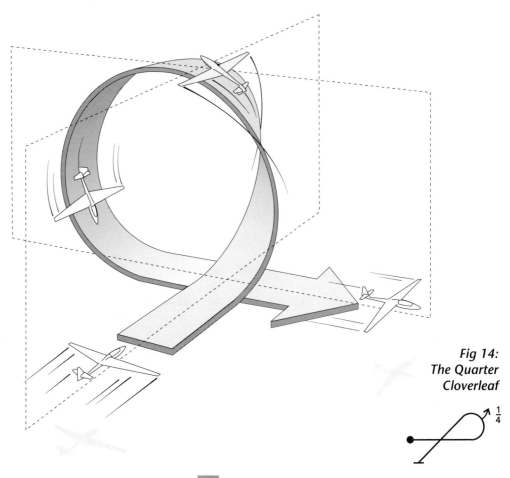

*Fig 14:*
*The Quarter*
*Cloverleaf*

$\frac{1}{4}$

pulling a minimum of **3g**. When the nose is 60–70° above the horizon and not before, glance along the wing in the direction of the roll (remembering that the exit line will be in the opposite direction). Pick a reference point on the horizon in line with the wingtip. Focus on this point and try not take your eyes off it. Move the stick in the same direction, rolling and pulling the glider towards this reference point. Be careful not to inadvertently relax the back-pressure on the stick when you start to roll, this is a very common fault.

As you pass through the inverted, stop the rolling as the nose lines up with the reference point, check that your wings are level and that you have changed direction by 90° from your entry line and continue with the rest of the Loop, ie. bring the nose through the reference point in a smooth line to intersect your initial ground line at 90°. If you are not properly lined up you can make corrections quite easily at this stage.

Complete the second half of the figure as for a Loop in the normal way to exit at the desired speed in horizontal flight. Your speed over the top should be slow, as in the Loop. If you notice it is too fast you either started pulling too hard when you began adding the rolling input or you initiated the roll too early.

In this case it may be better to roll out to the horizontal rather than complete the second half of the loop, and for this reason it is advisable to leave this figure until the roll is mastered.

## WARNING

**Starting the rolling action too soon, ie. before the nose is 60° above the horizon is likely to result in the glider reaching the inverted with too much speed for a safe looping exit. In this situation the best option is to continue rolling until back in erect flight**

The fixed undercarriage version of the fully aerobatic Pilatus B4. (*Mike Woollard*)

## The Half Flick Roll

This sounds like a complicated figure but in reality it is quite straight forward. The flick entry is almost a mechanical process requiring little finesse. Provided the appropriate control inputs are fed in correctly the result is more or less guaranteed. The second stage, the recovery, is not quite so simple and requires more skill and judgement in the exit.

From horizontal flight the glider should appear to flick quickly and without undue pitching up of the nose, on to its back. The rotation should stop accurately with the wings level and the nose will probably be pointing down 30–45°. The glider should proceed directly into the second half of a Loop to exit on a horizontal line.

**Common faults** are: not inducing a fully flicked rotation but using ailerons to roll the glider; not stopping the rotation with the wings level and so not finishing the looping component in a vertical plane.

**Target Speed** for a two-seater will typically be about 10–15 knots above the stall. It is important to establish a stabilised entry speed and attitude. Check that your wings are level, then simultaneously and rapidly apply full up elevator and full rudder. The control inputs should be very deliberate or a proper flick will not result. The ailerons should be kept in the neutral position. The glider will quickly rotate and the resulting rate of energy loss will be high, so high that after about 100° of rotation almost all speed and control effectiveness will have been lost. At this point momentarily apply full opposite rudder and move the stick forwards as for a spin recovery. Because of the slow speed it may take a moment for this to have an effect.

Check the ground line and as soon as the rudder starts to take effect stop the rotation on the line, level the wings with the horizon, using aileron if necessary, and centralise the controls, but keep the stick forward in order to regain flying speed before pulling out of the dive. Resist the temptation to pull back on the stick too early as you 'loop out' or a second 'flick' or a 'high speed stall' may result. As you pull out of the dive, monitor the ASI and adjust the elevator to give a smooth looping exit which is not too tight and which allows the speed to increase to the target entry speed you require in horizontal flight for the next figure.

**NB. Few gliders are cleared for this figure**

The two-seat Puchacz training glider, capable of flick manoeuvres. (*Mike Woollard*)

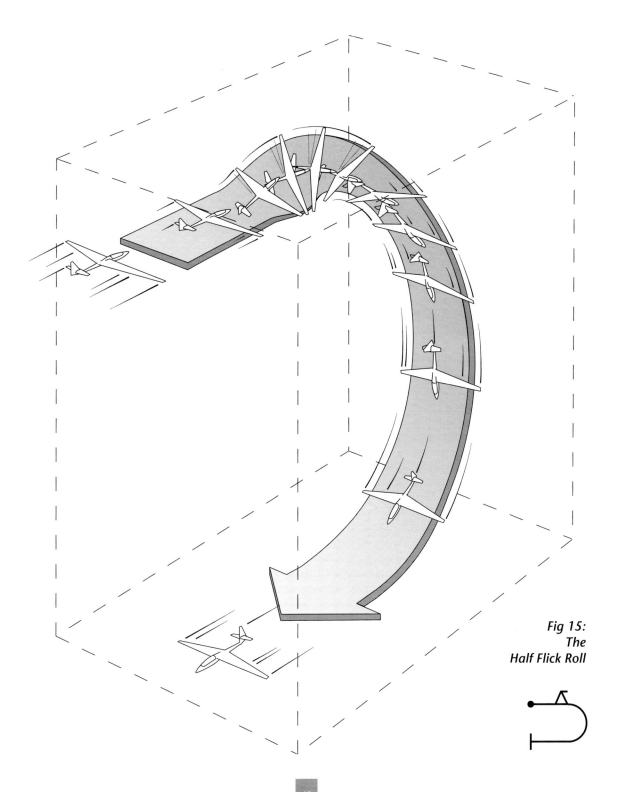

*Fig 15:*
*The*
*Half Flick Roll*

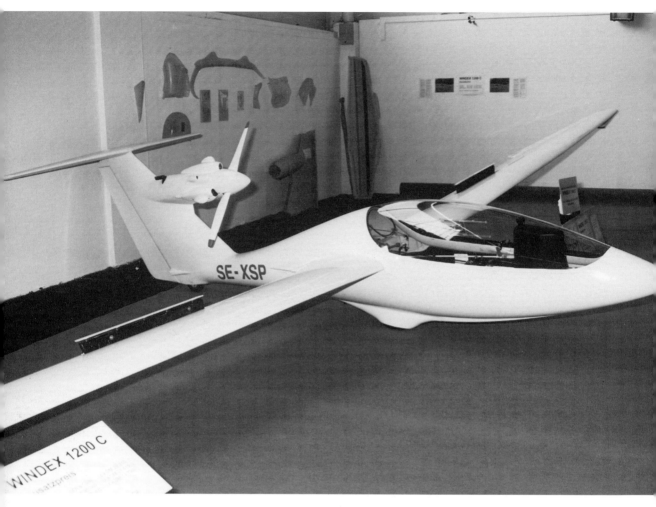

WINDEX 1200 C

SE-XSP

ABOVE:  The Windex 1200C fully aerobatic motor glider.  (*J. Ewald*)
OPPOSITE TOP:  The spacious cockpit of the Luñák.  (*Mike Woollard*)
OPPOSITE BELOW:  The prototype Polish Swift S1 'Unlimited' glider,
based on original Kobus design.  (*Guy Westgate*)

## The Humpty-Bump

This figure should start with a horizontal line followed by a vertical up-line. At the top there should be a small radius flown half loop. This may be specified either as over backwards or over forwards and is termed 'canopy down' or 'canopy up' accordingly (or 'wheels up' and 'wheels down' if you're American). This is followed by a vertical down-line and a horizontal exit line. The looping sections are CGT and must be wind corrected, but the two vertical lines are judged on fuselage angle or ZLA.

**Common faults** are: non-vertical lines and losing control by 'falling' over the top due to insufficient speed.

**Target speed** should be slightly higher than for a Loop in order to achieve a reasonable length up-line. From horizontal flight pull hard with a minimum of **3g** into a vertical climb. Stop at the vertical by checking a wingtip against the horizon or preferably a 'Wing Triangle' (see 'Training Key Points' at the beginning of Section B). Check that your wings are level and if possible pick a reference point vertically above you. Before you lose all flying speed pull or push over the top, flying a half loop. It is important to maintain flying speed throughout, but a minimum only. Too little speed and you will fall over the top.

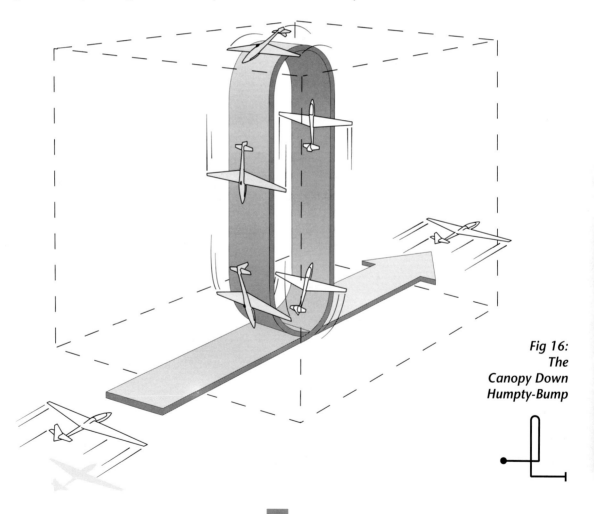

*Fig 16:*
*The*
*Canopy Down*
*Humpty-Bump*

The next step will depend on whether the figure is 'canopy up' or 'canopy down'. . .

## Canopy Down

This is in some ways the easier of the two since the ground is in view throughout, and the elevator is generally more powerful in the 'up' direction. Soon after you pass the inverted at the top you should start to move the stick forwards to keep the looping section looking 'round'. As soon as possible, check that your wings are level with the horizon and then, as the glider approaches the vertical, look along the wing for the reference triangle to stop the pitch down exactly at the vertical. This may need an abrupt check forward on the stick. Hold the vertical line for just a moment or there may be a risk of overspeeding in some types. Rotate immediately, pulling at least **3g** and monitor speed closely in order to exit to horizontal flight at the desired speed.

## Canopy Up

As the elevator in most gliders is generally more powerful in the 'up' direction, the elevator in the 'canopy up' Humpty is less effective. The pitching therefore needs to be initiated earlier to compensate for this, ie. at a higher airspeed. Push over the top, again flying a half loop without pushing more than zero **g**. As the horizon comes into view check wings level with the horizon. Check your alignment with the ground line as this comes into view and make sure you apply enough back pressure to stop the rotation when the nose is pointing vertically down, again referenced by looking at the wingtip. Hold the nose on a reference point again for a moment and recover from the dive as for 'canopy down'.

If you don't quite get the timing right and hold the up-line for too long, it is easy to find yourself in a tail-slide so be prepared to initiate the appropriate control action; hold all controls against their stops until reorientated to prevent slamming and possible damage.

*(See safety note on Tail-Slides in the next section on 'The Advanced Figures')*

SZD 59 'acro' – an 'Unlimited' aerobatic glider from Poland. *(J. Ewald)*

## The Stall Turn

The Stall Turn is very similar to the Humpty-Bump except that the change in direction at the top is achieved by a yawing rather than a pitching manœuvre. However, this does have one very useful effect; it produces a 180° change of heading, which is a convenient feature when devising programmes.

From a horizontal line the glider should pitch up smartly into the vertical, as for the Humpty. At the top it should pivot about one wingtip in a vertical plane at 90° to the entry line. This yawing motion should be smooth and symmetrical and ideally set about a point within the wingspan of the glider. The subsequent descent should be vertical followed by a crisp pitch up back to horizontal flight to finish in the opposite direction to the start of the figure. As with all vertical lines, they are judged on fuselage angle or ZLA to the horizon. The yaw over the top and the looping transition to and from horizontal flight are CGT related.

**Common faults**: Without doubt, this is one of the most difficult figures to get right in a glider. The point at which to initiate the yaw at the top is quite critical and is something which needs a great deal of practice, and in some gliders is difficult to predict. Another common problem is allowing a rolling element to creep into the yawing motion.

**Target Speed** is high again, typically not less than 100 knots, and ideally 110 knots. At lower speeds the up-line is simply not long enough and there is barely enough time to establish a vertical line before having to think about when to kick in the rudder.

From the horizontal, pull hard into the vertical. Pick a reference point on the horizon in line with the wingtip and in the intended direction of yaw. At the 'appropriate moment', ie. while you still have enough speed for rudder authority but not enough for any serious weathercock effect, apply full rudder in the direction of the turn-round. This 'appropriate moment' is one of the most difficult decisions in

aerobatics. Although it can be related to the ASI even this requires a great deal of practice on account of the considerable ASI lag brought about by rapid speed excursions. Fortunately, there are a few techniques which can help you out, which we shall look at in a moment.

From about 45° onwards during the first quarter of rotation it will be necessary to apply some 'opposite' aileron in order to counteract the secondary rolling effect of the yaw. In the last 90° quarter you will also have to apply some forward stick push in order to prevent the nose from coming 'up' as you approach the vertical down-line, ie. producing a less than vertical line. Also in the second quarter you will soon have to switch to opposite rudder in anticipation of the pendulum effect and rotational momentum which will try and swing the nose on past the vertical; ie. stopping the swing to the vertical should be 'dead beat'.

In order to keep the turn-round in one plane only and to ensure that this transforms smoothly into an accurate down-line, try and use the reference points. The wingtip and ground reference points are the key. As you yaw over the top, first the wingtip passes through the horizon point, then the nose follows through the same point. At the same time, the wing moves through the ground point below.

Finally, as you enter the vertical dive, the nose should pick up the ground reference point as the second wing passes through the horizon reference point. As usual, hold this down-line for a short time only then pull with at least **3g** into horizontal flight, carefully monitoring your speed.

## Some Useful Techniques for Stall Turns

These techniques can be invaluable for flying good Stall Turns and should be practised as soon as you begin to gain confidence. Unfortunately, there are some gliders in which even these tricks will not guarantee you success.

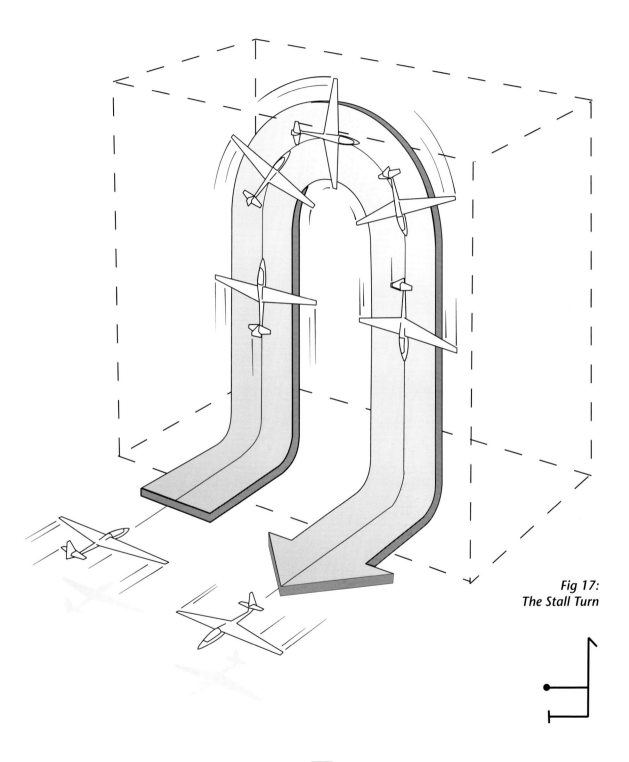

*Fig 17:*
*The Stall Turn*

### Increase rudder effectiveness

The first technique involves flying a deliberately yawed up-line. This cannot be too pronounced or it will 'show', ie. you would lose points in a competition, since it is the direction in which the glider is pointing that counts, ie. the Zero Lift Axis ZLA, not the flight path it is tracing.

As you rotate into the up-line include about ⅓ rudder deflection in the opposite direction to the intended turn-round, so that you fly a slightly yawed up-line. Hold this steady but remember to compensate for any secondary roll effect caused by using ailerons. This has the effect of making the rudder more effective when you do come to apply full rudder in the other direction for the yaw round.

Initially, it is a little difficult to purposefully 'cross' the controls during the pull to the vertical. In reality it may be easier to set 5° of bank before the pull-up. Then, after pulling to the vertical, apply rudder against the initial bank direction to keep the fuselage pointing straight up.

### Add aileron yawing moment

As the glider starts to yaw, briefly but positively move the stick fully in the aileron direction of the turn then back to the neutral position. This will have the effect of further enhancing the yaw due to the differential deflection of the ailerons. This is opposite to the effect you would expect in normal positive **g** flight. The reason for this is that, in normal horizontal flight, the up-going aileron is deflected into low pressure air and the down-going into high, and the differential angle of deflection ensures equal drag forces result on each aileron. In vertical flight and at such slow speed this pressure difference no longer exists and the up-going aileron, which is in the direction of the turn and which deflects further, simply creates more drag, providing a yawing moment in the direction in which we wish to go.

### Give the rudder a second kick

Finally, if you find the yawing begins to fizzle out too quickly because you have timed it wrong, move the rudder slowly to the fully 'opposite' position without causing any yaw in the wrong direction. Then, at the moment the glider starts to fall sideways, 'pump' the rudder hard once in the direction of the turn. This will be against the airflow over the tail area and will add an extra yawing impetus which may just save the situation. It may also improve the effectiveness of the rudder at this moment to position the elevator so it will have a minimum 'blanking' effect on the rudder.

> In the early days of practising this figure, using a 60° up-line rather than a 90° up-line will help one gain the necessary 'feel' before embarking upon a more vertical line.

OPPOSITE PAGE: A Pilatus B4 going vertical for a Stall Turn. (*Terry Joint*)

# 7 The Advanced Figures

## The Tail-Slide

You may be wondering what a Tail-Slide is doing in a list of aerobatic figures. You probably thought a Tail-Slide was what happened when things went wrong and was anyway to be avoided like the plague, along with the spin. It is in fact a recognised aerobatic figure.

There are two types of Tail-Slide. The first, which involves falling backwards over the top, is referred to as a 'Canopy Down' Tail-Slide and the second, where the fall-over is forwards, is called a 'Canopy Up' Tail-Slide. (Our American friends call these 'wheels up' and 'wheels down'). Each requires a slightly different technique.

In appearance the Tail-Slide consists of a rapid rotation from the horizontal into a vertical up-line, as for the Humpty and the Stall Turn. This line is held until all forward (vertical) speed is lost. The glider should then slide backwards down the same line for a discernible distance. The tail should then swing forwards or back, depending on the type of Tail-Slide, and the glider should rotate end for end so the nose finishes up pointing downwards. However, as the nose swings downwards it must, through the pendulum effect, swing past the vertical first by 20° or so before swinging back to the vertical, where it is held with no further swinging, for long enough only to establish a clear down-line. This is followed by rapid rotation with at least **3g** to the horizontal exit line.

It is important to realise that for competition flying the direction of 'fall' of the Tail-Slide will always be specified, hence the two separate figures. The nose swing past the vertical is there as proof that the glider really has fallen over the top and has not been flown over. If it is flown over, the pendulum effect does not occur.

**Common faults** are: Failing to maintain a vertical line, which is almost always due to the pilot's efforts to guarantee the 'fall-over' direction; not keeping the wings level throughout the figure; entry speed too slow, resulting in an up-line which is too short.

The key to this figure is a good long unyawed up-line using a high **target entry speed**. If there is any yaw in the up-line, the glider will drop a wing in the slide, which can be caught by using rudder towards the low wing (ie. the wrong way – remember we are flying backwards).

Start as for the Stall Turn and Humpty-Bump. From horizontal flight pull hard to a vertical line. As you near the top, and just before the elevator becomes ineffective, use the elevator to impart a very small pitching motion. This must not be enough to be visible from the ground but may help to ensure the fall-over direction. From this point a different procedure is followed for 'canopy up' and 'canopy down'…

### Canopy Down

At the zero speed point at the top the stick must be moved fully forward and held against the stops. This will ensure that the tail tends to swing out in the opposite direction to the intended fall-over as 'reverse' speed builds and the elevator begins to work in an opposite sense to normal (this is about the only time you will need to know how to fly backwards). As the fall-over becomes established keep the stick fully forward in order to limit how far the nose swings past the vertical. It will still swing well past the vertical but without the stick forward it will swing much too far.

As the nose then starts to swing back, move the stick back in order to 'catch' the nose at the vertical and hold it on a ground reference for just long enough to establish a vertical down-line. Then rotate smartly to horizontal flight as usual on the same heading as your entry line.

### Canopy Up

This time, at the zero speed point at the top, the stick must be held fully back against the stops to ensure the correct movement of the tail as you slide backwards. Hold the stick fully back until the glider has 'nosed over' and swung back past the vertical as far as it can go. (As before, the

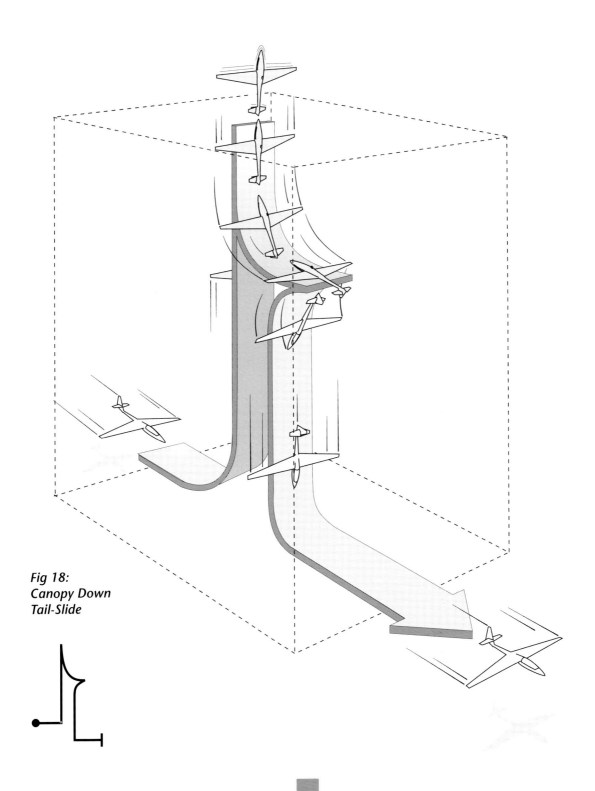

*Fig 18:*
*Canopy Down*
*Tail-Slide*

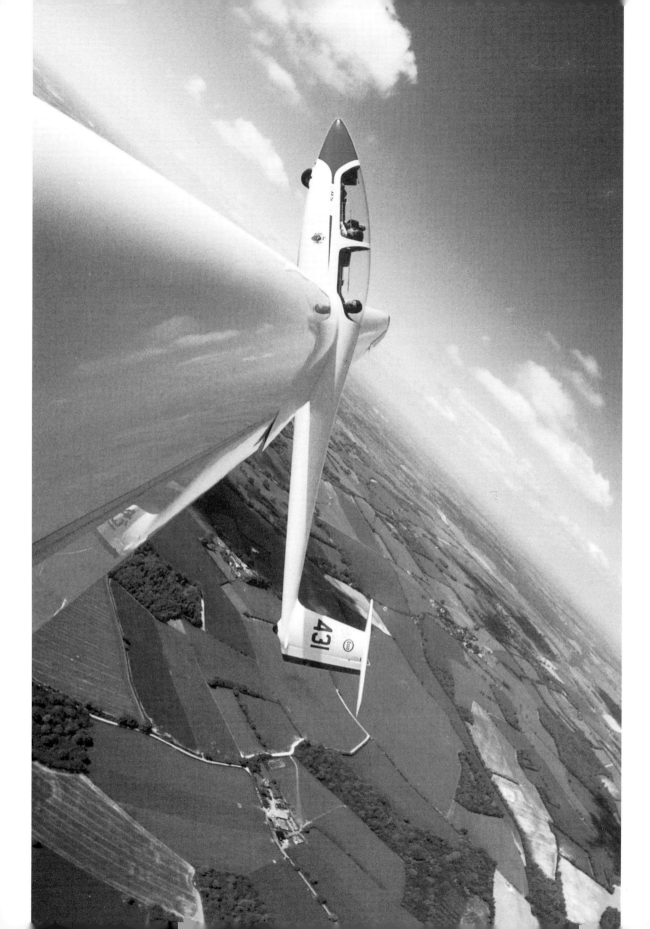

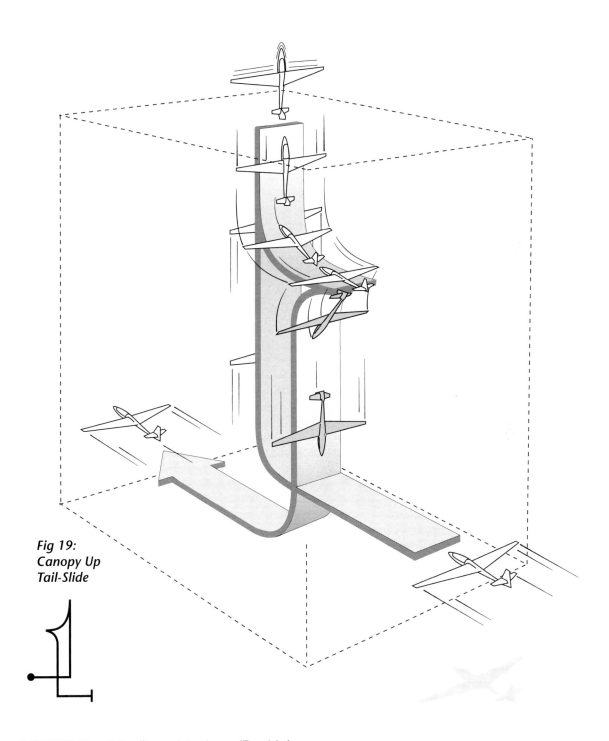

**Fig 19:**
**Canopy Up**
**Tail-Slide**

OPPOSITE PAGE: A K21 pulling up into a Loop. (*Terry Joint*)

elevator position will minimise this but the first time you try it the nose will swing what seems like an unnervingly long way.) Then move the stick quickly but progressively forwards sufficient to 'catch' the nose as it comes back to the vertical. Hold this for just long enough to establish a vertical down-line and pull hard again to horizontal flight, carefully monitoring speed and **g**.

The Tail-Slide is a very high scoring figure mainly because of the difficulty of guaranteeing the direction of the fall-over without jeopardising the appearance of the vertical line. If you do fall the wrong way and fly the alternative Tail-Slide perfectly you score an infuriating zero.

---

### TAIL-SLIDE CAUTION

*It is not possible to hold the controls neutral in a long Tail-Slide. The build up of forces becomes too great to hold, inevitably resulting in the control surfaces slamming aginst the stops with a serious likelihood of damage.*
*Once rearward movement is detected, hold the elevator against the up or down stop and brace the rudder and ailerons. If a long tail-slide develops, ensure ALL controls are braced against their stops.*

---

### The Inverted Flight

Inverted flight is physically very uncomfortable. For one thing the body's physiology is fundamentally affected; blood pressure reduces significantly and heart rate drops by a half. Add to this the pressures caused by the weight of your body hanging in the straps and you have a lot of physical discomfort. Not only that but soaring gliders are less stable upside-down and the control response can feel quite different. It is also very difficult to orientate upside-down since your brain is not very good at recognising what might be a familiar landscape when visual information is inverted. This and the peculiarity associated with blood and internal organs trying to get into your head results in an interesting and challenging experience. Holding just a simple inverted horizontal line becomes a very demanding task.

The benefits of thoroughly familiarising yourself with inverted flying before you start on the rolling manoeuvres cannot be overstated. It is well worth devoting a few flights to this in order to adjust to the unusual attitudes and forces involved. It would probably be even better value for money to do this in a Pitts or similar powered aircraft, given the limited time one can spend inverted in a glider in any one flight.

As with normal erect flight, the key to stable, accurate inverted flight is maintaining the correct steady attitude.

**Common faults** are not difficult to imagine from the above and include; non-stable attitude and speed, misuse of rudder and failing to keep your wings level.

**Target speed** is usually about 70–100 knots. The first thing to notice is that the 70 knot attitude is very nose high. This is partly due to the angle of incidence of the wings to the fuselage, the 'rigging angle' (in erect flight the fuselage actually points slightly nose down when the wing root chord is horizontal) and partly due to the greater angle of attack required to produce the same amount of lift when the wing is working (less efficiently) upside-down. 70 knots may seem like a high speed until you realise that the inverted stalling speed is probably not much less than 60. Try and keep one eye on your reference point and avoid large elevator inputs or you may soon find yourself 'dolphining' badly. At speeds less than 65 knots, lateral instability can be quite a problem and in most gliders will be difficult to contain below 60.

Inverted flying techniques are just the same as for erect flight so remember to fly by attitude. 'Chasing' the ASI may have an even worse effect than it does in erect flight.

Some gliders' ASIs will misread when flying inverted due to pressure errors caused by the fuselage's inverted attitude. A pitot tube extension (as used on the ASK21) may be required to give correct readings. Check with the flight manual before flying.

## The Half Slow Roll (from Inverted to Erect)

Your first experience of this figure will probably be in the recovery from a demonstration of inverted flight. This in turn is most likely to be in preparation for rolling and your instructor may encourage you to take the controls for this manœuvre. It is quite easy to perform and will immediately give you confidence about your ability to recover from inverted flight by rolling.

Because this figure is likely to be your first encounter with any form of rolling we have described it first, but it is important to read the following in conjunction with the notes on the next figure, the Full Slow Roll, where you will find a detailed examination of the whole rolling process.

From the horizontal inverted line this figure should involve a half roll to erect flight with no more movement of the nose from the centre line than is necessary, and without the nose moving too far below the horizon. The half roll should stop with the wings level and with the glider on the original heading. This figure is judged CGT so corrections for wind effects may be made.

**Common faults** are: exit off line, often by a long way, after insufficient pushing away from the centre line at the knife-edge, and the nose swinging too far below the horizon.

**Target speed** is typically 75–100 knots. You have completed an inverted line with the nose about 20° above the horizon. First choose a good reference point ahead then without lowering the nose unduly, apply full aileron promptly. Be sure to keep the stick hard over. At the same time maintain forward pressure on the stick and **pay very careful attention to the nose/horizon relationship and your reference point**.

As you start the roll, almost full opposite rudder will help control the huge adverse yaw. Then, as you roll past the 45° point this must be changed to 'top' rudder to try and prevent the nose from sliding down towards the horizon as you approach the knife-edge. You won't be able to prevent this happening but without the rudder input the nose will swing much further below the horizon. As you approach the knife-edge push the stick forwards to move the nose

*Fig 20:*
*Half Slow Roll from Inverted to Erect Flight*

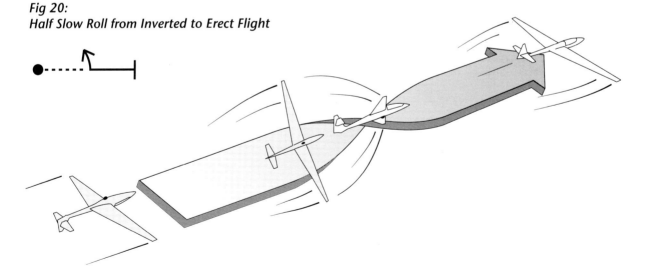

away from the reference point by 30° or so. This is necessary because in the last quarter the glider is bound to slide sideways and down in a 'dishing' or 'barrelling' movement which will result in a considerable heading change. This cannot be avoided and can only be compensated for by 'pushing off line' in anticipation of the swing back. By the time you reach the 100° point you should begin to pull back on the stick in an effort to keep the nose up as much as possible. The 'barrelling' should finish with the wings level and the nose will probably be about 30° below the horizon, but now back on line. Pull up to regain horizontal flight and complete a horizontal line.

## CAUTIONARY NOTE

*The Rolling manoeuvre is important because it facilitates a safe route from inverted back to erect flight.*

*Unless carefully planned and set up, a return to erect flight by completing the loop must be avoided as it is a potential death trap. Inverted flight involves speeds in excess of 80 knots. With the additional 65–75 knots which will develop in a pull through, maximum speeds can be reached or exceeded very easily. This is particularly relevant to students learning to roll and fly inverted. When things go wrong, there can be a great temptation to return to erect flight by pulling rather than rolling. In such cases, inverted flying speeds are likely to be excessively high, making the pull through option very dangerous indeed*

*REMEMBER:*

*ALWAYS PUSH AND ROLL OUT from inverted flight*

In your first attempts at this figure it is best not to try and compensate too hard for the barrelling off line but merely to notice how far off line the nose swings when you don't. The rudder may be kept neutral throughout with only the axis correction elevator push used at the knife edge position. Eventually, as you become more familiar with rolling, the correct use of rudder may be introduced to improve the figure by reducing the 'barrelling' effect.

### The Full Slow Roll

The Slow Roll is sometimes referred to as the 'Axial Roll'. A true Axial Roll, however, is impossible to achieve in most gliders. Even a reasonably axial Roll is difficult with a slow roll rate and requires considerable expertise. The C of G of the glider will inevitably make excursions about the axis but to a much lesser extent than in a Barrel Roll which is a completely different figure.

From a ground observer's point of view, the glider should appear to roll at a constant rate through 360° without unnecessary pitching or swinging of the nose either up or down or to either side. A certain amount of barrelling in the final quarter is unavoidable as we have seen, especially in the majority of two-seaters. This is therefore acceptable, provided it is kept to a minimum using the technique described above. Exit should be on a horizontal line on the original heading. As with all rolling figures, the glider flight path is judged CGT.

**Common faults** are: pitching up too high on entry; too much barrelling in the last quarter; not pushing the nose off line enough at the final knife-edge to compensate for the dishing and heading change in the last quarter; not maintaining full aileron.

The beginner may find the Full Slow Roll somewhat easier to fly than the Half Roll to Inverted; having simply to hold full aileron throughout the inverted stage of the Full Roll leaves you with more time to concentrate on the crucial tasks of controlling the nose position and later, the appropriate use of rudder. It is essential to look ahead and monitor the nose's position relative to the horizon and ensure that it follows the correct path.

### The Rolling Process Explained

Now let's examine the rolling process in detail so

Views around the roll.
(*Guy Westgate*)

*Fig 21:*
*The Full Slow Roll*

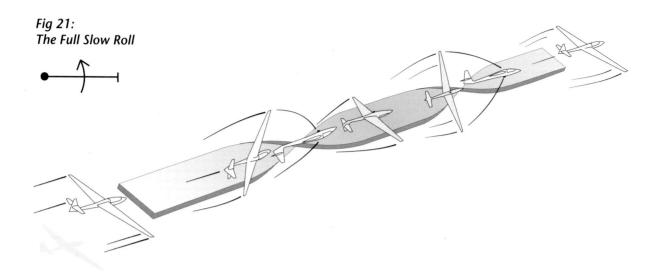

you will have a better idea of what you are trying to do. We should start by looking at the Lift Coefficient ($C_L$) Diagram, ie. the graph which shows us the relationship between the $C_L$ and the Angle of Attack of the wing:

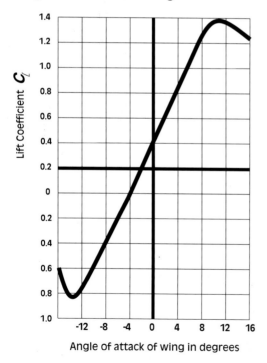

*Fig 22: The Lift Coefficient Diagram*

We can see from the $C_L$ Diagram for a soaring glider that we are producing positive lift even at small negative angles of attack. To produce appreciable negative lift we have to achieve quite large negative angles of attack, even at high speeds.

This, combined with the rigging angle of the wings, means that in steady **1g inverted flight** the nose of the glider will tend to be quite high compared to the attitude required in erect flight see Fig 23.

Now let's look at the view we are expecting to see ahead of us as we progress around the roll . . .

### Vertical Reference Points for the Roll

To start with, Fig 24 shows the points where the nose of the glider should be when erect and inverted. Now let's add on the intermediate points as we pass the two knife-edges, Fig 25. In this position the wings will be producing no lift and the glider will experience **0g**. The combination of asymmetric wing section and rigging angle means that when the right wing is down in knife-edge flight the nose should be deflected to the left, and when the left wing is down the nose should be deflected to the right . . .

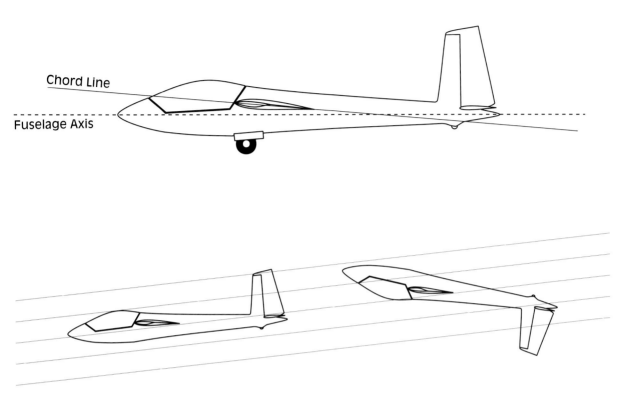

Fig 23: Flight Attitude in Erect and Inverted Flight

Fig 24: Vertical Reference Points for the Roll

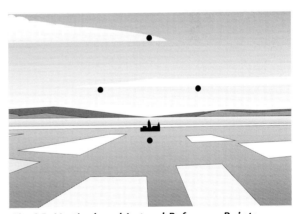

Fig 25: Vertical and Lateral Reference Points

If we join these points and all the intermediate points we end up with a 'sacred circle' as first described by Pohorely and referred to by Müller and Carson in their book *Flight Unlimited* (Ref 6). This is the theoretical path which should be 'drawn' by the glider as it performs an axial roll.

We now have a picture for a straight roll at **1g** all the way round, Fig 26. Unfortunately, we can't actually fly this in our glider without adding another set of wings at right angles to the ones we already have to produce our **1g** as we pass knife-edge, so we shall have to modify our expectations to suit the real world.

The Swift S1. (*Guy Westgate*)

*Fig 26: The Sacred Circle*

We shall now describe a roll to the right. To start with, we shall treat it as two half rolls with a pause inverted. As we will be producing on average less than **1g** during the first half roll we shall have to start with the nose somewhat higher than ideal and accept that it will be somewhat lower than ideal at the end.

To fly a straight line however, we still need the nose to be offset to the left at knife-edge. This means the nose will now follow the line of a half ellipse rather than a half circle. After completing the first half of the roll we then push the nose up to the correct position relative to the horizon to maintain steady inverted flight.

*Fig 27: Visual References Rolling to Inverted Flight*

We shall now complete the roll back to erect. Again we'll be producing less than **1g** so must start with the nose higher and expect it to finish lower. In the final quarter of the roll we shall be

pulling to prevent the nose from dropping too much, thereby pulling it back towards our ideal straight line. In anticipation of this we therefore usually push a little further off line as we approach the second knife-edge than would seem ideal. We thus end up with a semi-circular movement of the nose.

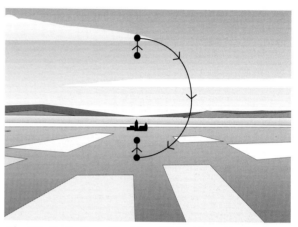

*Fig 28: Path Described by Glider Nose Rolling from Inverted to Erect Flight*

Once we have mastered the roll in two parts we'll join them together. We obviously do not want to have a pause in the middle while we raise the nose so we combine the two halves in one continuous smooth movement. The result is that the nose describes a spiral motion thus . . .

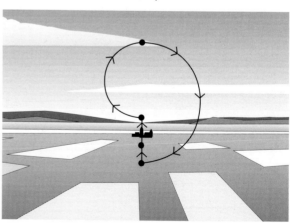

*Fig 29 Path Described by Glider Nose during the Full Roll*

A 25-metre ASH 25 pulling up into a wing-bending Loop. (*Tony Hutchins*)

So much for what we are looking for. How do we achieve it? Let's look at each control separately...

### Ailerons

Ailerons are the easiest to consider. Our two-seater trainers roll so slowly that there is little scope for finesse. If we want the roll to continue and we are at or below $V_a$, then we use full ailerons. When we want it to stop we centralise them. It's as simple as that. However, if things are not going quite as planned you will find there is a natural instinct to slow down events by reducing aileron deflection. This temptation must be resisted. During the roll the stick is either hard over or central. We cannot afford any half measures.

At various stages in the roll, the roll rate will be modified by the varying effectiveness of the ailerons caused by aileron differential and adverse yaw effects. It is not uncommon for some gliders to autorotate from inverted to erect flight, in which case the roll rate increases and some compensating reduction in aileron deflection may be appropriate.

### Elevator

At the start of all rolling manoeuvres, especially during early training, the elevator will be used to pitch the nose up 15° or more. This will allow for the universal tendency of all students to let the the nose fall too far below the horizon in the first and second quarters of the roll.

During the first half of the roll the elevator should be moved smoothly from a position which gives +1g at the start, to zero **g** at knife-edge, then −1g when inverted, ie. the stick moves forward. In the second half the reverse process is applied; smoothly from −1g to start with, through zero **g** at knife-edge, to finish at +1g. Be careful not to jerk the elevator. This can be quite uncomfortable and looks bad to an observer. A harsh push when inverted can also produce a stall and possibly an inverted flick or spin.

### Rudder

This is the control which requires real judgement. In general, the less the rudder is used the less will be the drag produced and less energy will be lost during the figure. Quite a reasonable approximation to a straight roll can be flown with the rudder held central, and this is what beginners are taught to do. However, we are aiming for perfection...

As we start the roll (a roll to the right) adverse yaw will cause the nose to swing up and to the left. Exactly where we want it to go. As we progress towards the knife-edge we find we must progressively introduce more left rudder to keep the nose rising, but then reduce it somewhat as we approach inverted. From inverted, adverse yaw is working against us and we need left rudder to make the nose swing in the direction we want it to go. As we progress towards knife-edge for the second time our problem is now that the nose wants to drop, so we remove the left rudder and smoothly apply right rudder, which is now 'top rudder'.

This movement of the rudder from one side to the other between the inverted and the final knife-edge is a surprisingly difficult undertaking for the novice but is one which cannot be overlooked if a good roll is to be achieved.

As we progress through the last quarter we steadily ease back on the stick to prevent the nose from dropping too far. At the same time maintain sufficient right rudder only to help prevent the nose from swinging to the left; not so much as to cause obvious yawing to the left. The nose should stop on the original line with the rudder central and should then be raised to regain straight and level flight.

The above control movements are a guideline only. It is more important to have a clear picture of what you expect to see and use the controls harmoniously to achieve that picture.

The most common fault with early attempts is reverting to soaring technique and not allowing the adverse yaw to swing the nose away from the direction of roll at the start. If this does happen, stop the roll immediately as the nose will be low throughout the roll causing over-speed problems. Regain your speed and attitude in erect flight and then try again.

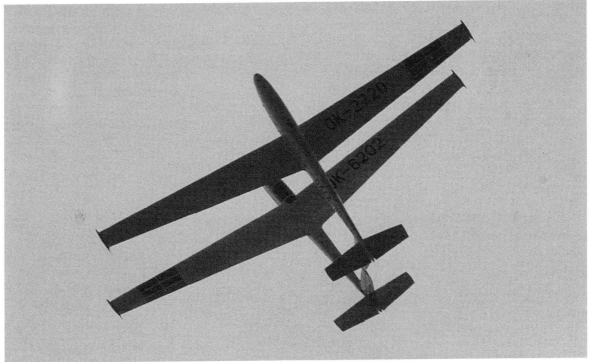

TOP:  Akaflieg München Mü-28 – fully aerobatic glider with manual or automatic controlled flaps. (*J. Ewald*)
ABOVE:  Mirror formation. (*J. Ewald*)

## The Half Slow Roll (to Inverted Flight)

From a horizontal line the glider should be seen to roll at a constant rate, with minimum pitching of the nose, along the same axis as the entry line. After 180° the roll should stop as crisply as possible with wings level. Finally, an inverted horizontal line should be flown on the same axis and for the same distance as the entry line.

As with all rolling figures, the rolling is judged on the centre of gravity track of the glider (CGT), not on the fuselage angle, but the lines before and after the roll are judged zero lift axis (ZLA).

**Common faults** are: not maintaining the correct nose/horizon relationship for each stage of the roll and exiting from the half roll off line with wings not level or with incorrect inverted attitude.

**Target Speed** is typically 80–100 knots. From horizontal flight with wings level and no yaw, select a reference point on or near the horizon. Raise the nose to 15° above the horizon and immediately use full aileron to roll the glider. To start with, when learning this figure it is probably better, as already described in the Half Roll to Erect, not to try and include any rudder inputs; rather keep the rudder in the neutral position. In particular, and as described for the Full Roll, be careful not to apply rudder, out of habit, in the direction of roll or you may pull the nose down below the horizon by the knife-edge. (Later you will find that it is useful to start applying 'top' rudder as you near the 90° point as already mentioned, but to start with this may only complicate matters.)

While focusing your attention on the position of the nose in relation to the horizon, roll through the first quarter. As you reach the knife-edge begin to move the stick forwards and as the wings pass through the knife-edge continue to increase the forward pressure, carefully monitoring the position of the nose. By the 135° point the stick should be well forward ready to hold the nose up above the horizon in inverted flight. This requires a surprising amount of force. Stop the roll with the wings level and hold the nose at an attitude of about 20° above the horizon, sufficient to give an airspeed of less than 90 knots. Immediately look for the ASI (you'll be surprised how difficult it is to find when you are upside-down). Notice your sink rate; probably 4 knots at least (gliders don't soar very well upside-down). Notice also how nose up the 'normal' attitude is and how difficult it is to maintain accurate speed control. Finally, check the glider's orientation with selected reference points making corrections as necessary. It is probably wise to roll out again after a few seconds, particularly in the early stages of inverted flying, to minimise the effects of physical exertion which could affect your ability to recover to erect flight.

*Fig 30:*
*The Half Slow Roll (to Inverted Flight)*

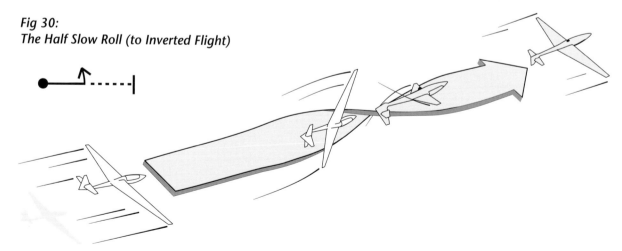

## The Half Cuban Eight

This is a figure which flown twice gives the Full Cuban Eight, but for training purposes we shall deal only with the Half Cuban Eight.

The first ⅝ of this figure should look the same as a Loop. After the inverted point the nose is allowed to come down to a 45° down-line and the wings are momentarily held level by checking forward with the stick. A half roll to erect flight then follows immediately. This should stop cleanly with wings level and the 45° down-line re-established. The figure is then completed by rotating back to horizontal flight on a reciprocal heading to the entry line.

However, because of the slow roll rate and limiting $V_a$ and $V_{ne}$ of most two-seaters it is not usually possible to fly this figure with a true 45° down-line and remain within the Flight Envelope. In training we should therefore use a 30° down-line in order to provide a safety margin.

As with the Chandelle, the down-lines need only be established, not held. If they are held they must be of equal length either side of the roll. Because of its low $V_{ne}$ the holding of the down-lines is best omitted altogether when flying the Puchacz, and the use of a 30° down-line slope is advisable to keep the speed under control.

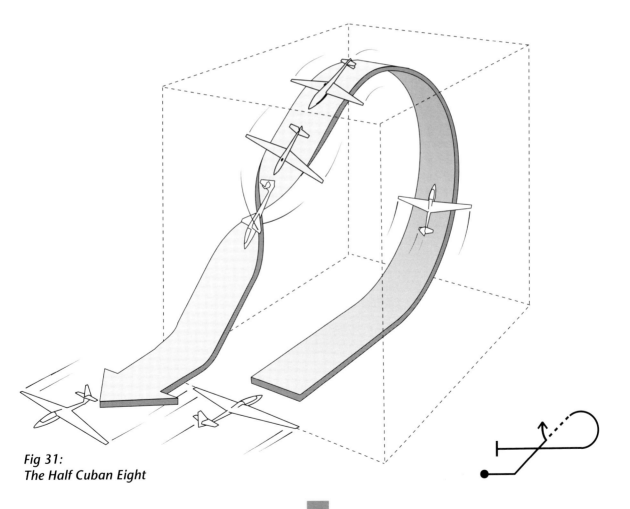

*Fig 31:*
*The Half Cuban Eight*

**Common faults** are: not maintaining an accurate down-line throughout the rolling phase, often resulting in a serious build-up of speed; exiting off line, and misuse of the rudder during the rolling process.

**Target speed** is as for the Loop. This figure should start in exactly the same way as a Loop. As you pass the inverted, instead of only briefly relaxing back-pressure, look ahead and down for the ground line and check with forward stick to stop the rotation momentarily when the correct downline angle is achieved. (Check wingtip for this angle and pick a reference point ahead to hold this line.) Immediately start to roll with full aileron and some opposite rudder in order to prevent the nose from lowering and swinging further.

*Tip: Using two hands on the stick during the rolling process can help ensure the stick is not inadvertently pulled back during the roll, causing a steepening of the down-line and an undesirable speed increase.*

At the knife-edge position, push the nose off line as you would for the half roll and reverse the rudder to the 'top' for the last quarter.

Stop the roll after half a turn with the wings level and the nose still on the down-line reference point. Because this roll from inverted to erect is on a down-line the barrelling effects are less pronounced than on a horizontal line. The need for corrective measures is therefore much reduced. Press on with all the procedures in the down-line without any delay or speed will increase rapidly. It may be difficult to complete the figure without excessive speed. Throughout this figure it is important to bear in mind the Flight Envelope limitations associated with the use of aileron and elevator when used together.

*(See the section on Flight Envelopes for more information on this.)*

## The 360° Inverted Turn

If you find inverted straight and level flight difficult, wait till you try turning . . .

The same criteria apply to inverted turns as to erect. After a horizontal section the glider should roll smartly to a 60° angle of bank. This should be an accurately maintained constant radius turn, well co-ordinated and with a roll out on the original heading.

**Common faults** result mainly from inaccurate speed control and flying at less than a 60° angle of bank. Poor coordination is often seen because of the reversed control inputs required when inverted

**Target speed** is typically 80–90 knots. At speeds less than this, speed control and co-ordination are more difficult. At higher speeds height loss is the penalty. This becomes critical in competition flying.

The first time you attempt an Inverted Turn you will probably find that the glider will go in the 'wrong' direction. You may not have realised that the control inputs for erect flight work fine in inverted flight and even roll the glider in the same direction, but the down-going wing in erect flight is now the up-going wing inverted, and hence produces a turn direction opposite to the side you move the stick towards. It's difficult enough visualising this when sitting upright in your armchair let alone when hanging upside down in your glider. But don't despair, there is a neat trick which short-cuts the thinking process; simply initiate the turn with a bit of rudder. The rudder works in the same sense, as far as your feet think at least. As usual, the yaw will produce some secondary roll and all will become clear. You just move the stick further in that direction of roll. In fact, it will then appear that you are moving the stick in the opposite direction to the rudder, but this doesn't pose quite the problem you would think. Of course, viewed from above, all the control surfaces are doing just what they do in erect flight.

Having successfully rolled to a 60° banked turn, maintain speed and co-ordinate in the usual way. The yaw string works nearly as well as in erect flight but don't look at the Turn and Slip ball if you have one; the curved glass tube is now the wrong way up. There is a tendency always to monitor speed using the ASI when inverted. Do watch your attitude. Also don't forget lookout and if you have trouble navigating because the world looks completely unrecognisable try and relate to one or two large key landmarks only; the sun can be an indispensable position marker. Look for your ground line and roll out on the original heading.

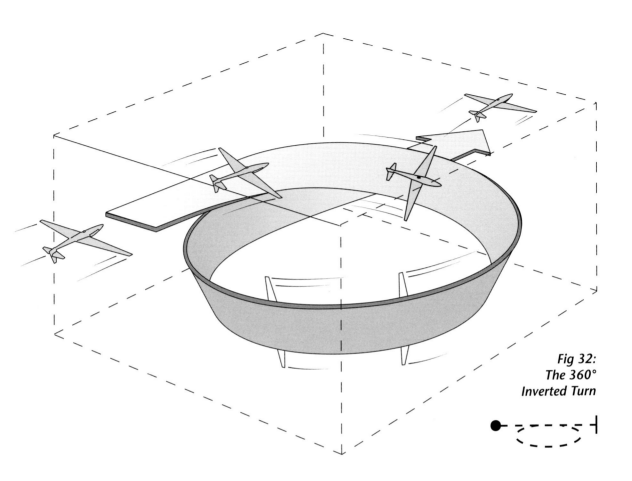

*Fig 32:*
*The 360°*
*Inverted Turn*

## The Pull-Through from Inverted Flight

In the foregoing text much emphasis has been placed on the dangers associated with pulling through, or completing the loop whilst inverted, due to the extreme speed build-up which can result. It may therefore come as something of a surprise to find this manoeuvre now being introduced here as part of an advanced figure. It is important that the aerobatic pilot under training learns to recover instinctively from inverted flight by rolling rather than the hitherto more natural pull-through. Once this instinctive appreciation has been attained then the judicious use of the pull-through manoeuvre can be introduced.

A looping Pull-Through from Inverted Flight is indeed a safe and legitimate manoeuvre provided

it is done correctly. It will be seen performed by any pilot practising for, or performing in, an intermediate level competition, so this text would not be complete without addressing this figure in full. It is quite safe to perform PROVIDED THE GLIDER IS SLOWED TO ITS MINIMUM POSSIBLE INVERTED FLYING SPEED before the pull-through manoeuvre is executed. Inverted flight normally occurs at typically 80/90 knots for a glider with an inverted stall speed of 55/65 knots. With a 60-knot speed gain likely in the pull-through from inverted flight, the difference between the inverted stall speed and normal inverted flying speeds is fundamental to keeping the glider speed safely below $V_{ne}$.

From inverted flight with level wings, the glider must be slowed gradually to a **target**

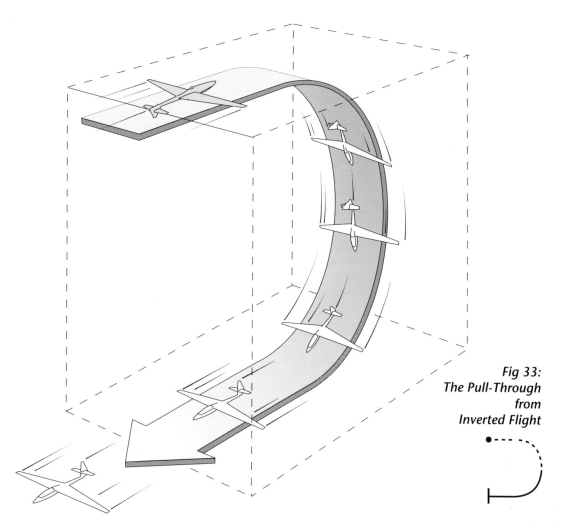

*Fig 33:*
*The Pull-Through*
*from*
*Inverted Flight*

**speed** just above the inverted stall speed with great care being taken to ensure that there is no rudder deflection and therefore no yaw present which could start an inverted spin entry. From this point the pull-through is exactly the same as for the second half of the normal Loop but ensuring that adequate **g** loads are pulled to control the speed. A pull-out of no less than **3g** but ideally **4g** should be used in this looping exit, which will typically result in an exit speed approaching 120 knots. Such a figure is not therefore to be recommended on a glider with a low $V_{ne}$ such as the Puchacz with its 116-knot limit, and since the glider will be flying well above $V_a$, care in handling the controls is obviously required.

**Common faults** are: pushing the nose up too quickly to slow the inverted flying speed with the result that the stall may be reached prematurely. An unsightly up-slope may also result. Not maintaining level wings and flying with some rudder/yaw present all compound the difficulty of flying this figure. It is also possible to enter a deep stall with a high rate of descent as evidenced on the variometer, in which case it is best to regain 20 knots of inverted flying speed, roll out and then try again.

During the pull-through pick up your reference line as you would in a Loop and correct for any misalignment by introducing a small amount of roll as necessary. Such correction should be so small as to be imperceptible to a ground observer.

In the event of an inverted spin commencing, a positive recovery is required. Correct any yawing action with rudder and then pull back on the stick with centralised rudder to return to horizontal flight in a looping pull-through.

## The Reverse Half Cuban Eight

Another inverted pull-through figure which will commonly be seen, is the Reverse Half Cuban Eight often called the 'Split S'. This has the same shape as the Half Cuban Eight but with the glider flown in the opposite direction through the figure. The half roll is performed on the 45° up-line before the looping pull-through is flown.

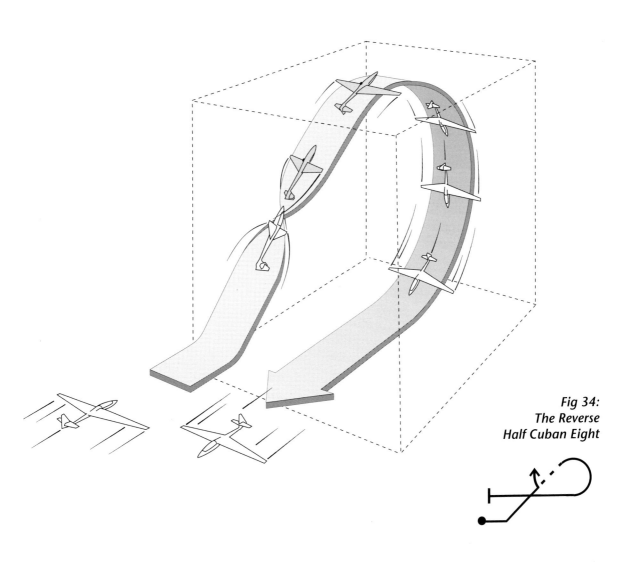

Fig 34:
The Reverse
Half Cuban Eight

**Common faults** are: not having enough entry speed before establishing the 45° up-line. The airspeed and roll rate then both diminish too rapidly for the glider to achieve wings level inverted flight before the pull becomes required. It is important to achieve a true 45° up-line before rolling commences, since too shallow a line can result in too high an airspeed when inverted for a safe pull-through to be made. As with the previous figure, great care is required to ensure that the inverted speed is sufficiently slow to enable the looping pull-through to be safely achieved. If this is in doubt, a rolling recovery to horizontal flight is the safest course of action . . .

**Target speed** is typically 20 knots higher than for the Loop entry speed, in the region of 120 knots. Pitch up to the 45° up-line checking with the wingtip triangle before using the MAXIMUM ALLOWABLE rolling action for the indicated airspeed. Since the rolling action is likely to commence at a speed above $V_a$, progressive aileron deflection is required, maintaining a constant roll rate. Begin with no more than half deflection, increasing to full deflection after a quarter roll. At this point the glider will have slowed to below $V_a$, which it will do fairly quickly given its upward path and the slowing effect of the deflected ailerons. It is important to maintain the 45° up-slope axis during the roll. A suitable forward reference point such as part of a cloud formation can assist this process.

As the inverted position is reached, check the wings are level and assess the airspeed. If possible, push forward on the stick to maintain the 45° up slope for a moment to allow the airspeed to reduce almost to the inverted stall speed. Then pull back to effect the looping pull-out, in the same way as for the second half of a normal Loop. During the pull-out, pick up your ground reference line and correct for any deviations which have occurred during the earlier part of the figure.

In practice, when this figure is flown in most two-seat training gliders, the inverted position will be achieved at a very low airspeed (even below the normal stalling speed) and similar to the conditions often experienced at the top of a Loop. It will therefore require an immediate pull-through back to horizontal flight.

## 8 Sample Programmes to Fly

In learning the previous figures you will inevitably have flown short sequences of figures and will be quite familiar with the concept of their representation as an Aresti diagram drawn on a trusty 'Post-it' pad. It is important that figures in a sequence are compatible with one another. For example, a Half Cuban Eight needs to follow a speed-gaining figure such as a spin, with perhaps a 45⁰ up-line to finish as shown below.

We now extend this idea of a sequence to perhaps 10 or 12 figures in an aerobatic programme. The simpler sequences for beginners are flown between 3000 and 1200ft, whereas the more advanced sequences begin at 4000ft.

Outlined on the next few pages are a number of programmes of increasing difficulty which you might like to try before devising your own. And beware of the technically impossible sequence which some pilots leave on their instrument panel just to impress the uninitiated!

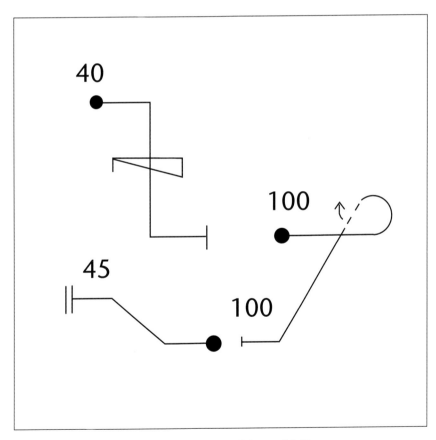

Simple Aerobatic Sequence of Compatible Figures.

ABOVE: Pete Mallinson holding the Puchacz in inverted flight. (*Guy Westgate*)
LEFT: Layout of a typical aerobatic 'box'. (*Guy Westgate*)

## Sequence 1

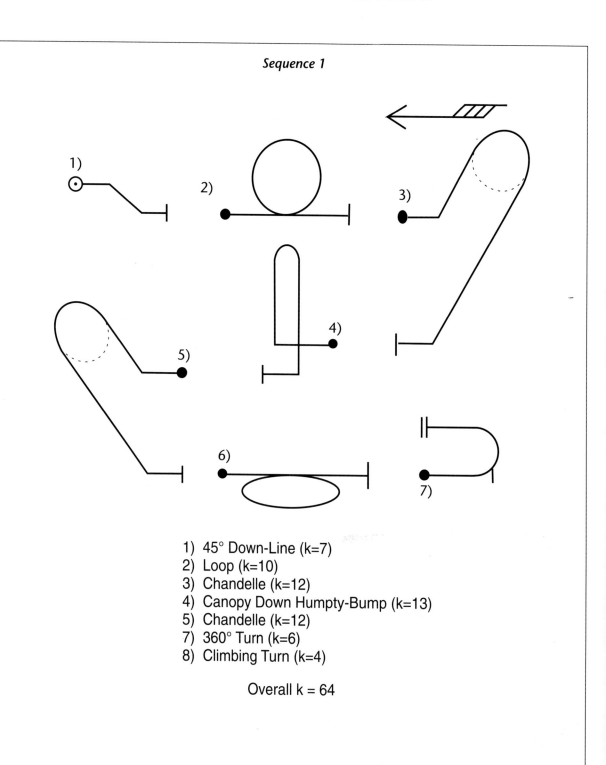

1) 45° Down-Line (k=7)
2) Loop (k=10)
3) Chandelle (k=12)
4) Canopy Down Humpty-Bump (k=13)
5) Chandelle (k=12)
7) 360° Turn (k=6)
8) Climbing Turn (k=4)

Overall k = 64

## Sequence 2

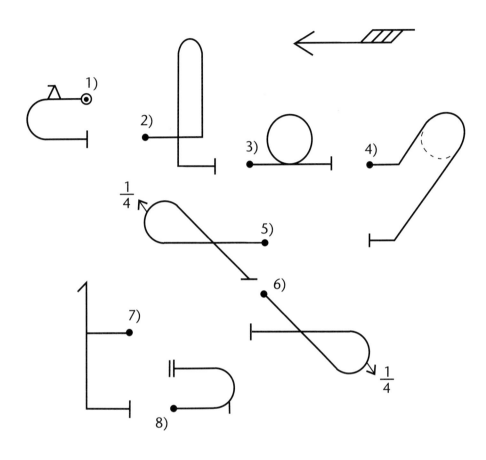

1) Flick Half Roll (k=18)
2) Canopy Down Humpty-Bump (k=13)
3) Loop (k=10)
4) Chandelle (k=12)
5) Quarter Cloverleaf (k=16)
6) Quarter Cloverleaf (k=16)
7) Stall Turn (k=17)
8) Climbing Turn (k=4)

Overall k = 106

An inverted Fox flanked by two Swift S1s. (*Beat Schück*)

## Sequence 3

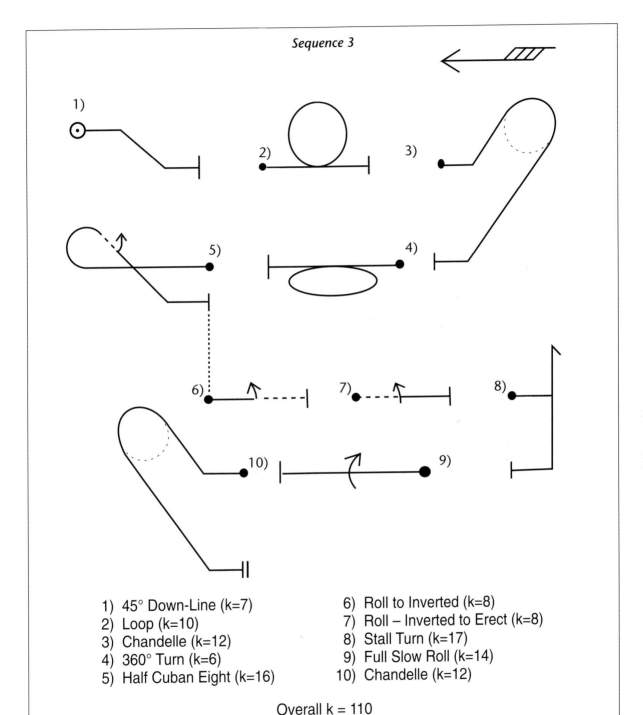

1) 45° Down-Line (k=7)
2) Loop (k=10)
3) Chandelle (k=12)
4) 360° Turn (k=6)
5) Half Cuban Eight (k=16)

6) Roll to Inverted (k=8)
7) Roll – Inverted to Erect (k=8)
8) Stall Turn (k=17)
9) Full Slow Roll (k=14)
10) Chandelle (k=12)

Overall k = 110

## Sequence 4

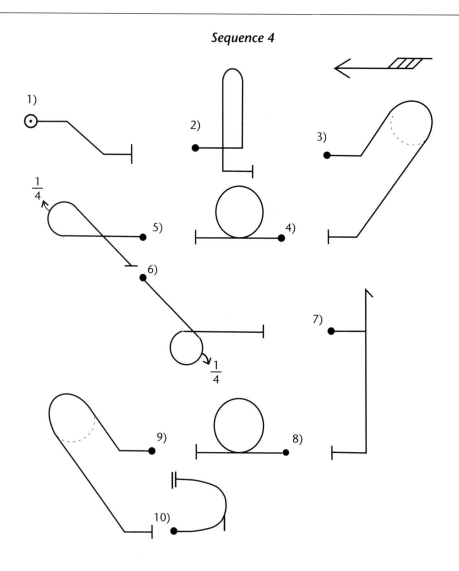

1) 45° Down-Line (k=7)
2) Canopy Down Humpty-Bump (k=13)
3) Chandelle (k=12)
4) Loop (k=10)
5) Quarter Cloverleaf (k=16)
6) Quarter Cloverleaf (k=16)
7) Stall Turn (k=17)
8) Loop (k=10)
9) Chandelle (k=12)
10) Climbing Turn (k=4)

Overall k = 117

State-of-the-Art 'Unlimited' aerobatic gliders waiting to compete. (*Beat Schück*)

## Sequence 5

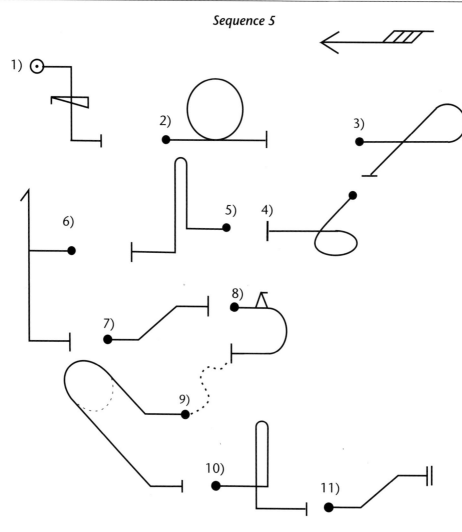

1) 1 Turn Spin (k=14)
2) Loop (k=10)
3) Quarter Cloverleaf (k=16)
4) 270° Turn (k=5)
5) Canopy Up Humpty-
   Bump (k=15)
6) Stall Turn (k=17)

7) 45° Up-Line (k=7)
8) Half Flick Roll (k=18)
9) Chandelle (k=12)
10) Canopy Down Humpty-
    Bump (k=13)
11) 45° Up-Line (k=7)

Overall k = 134

## Sequence 6

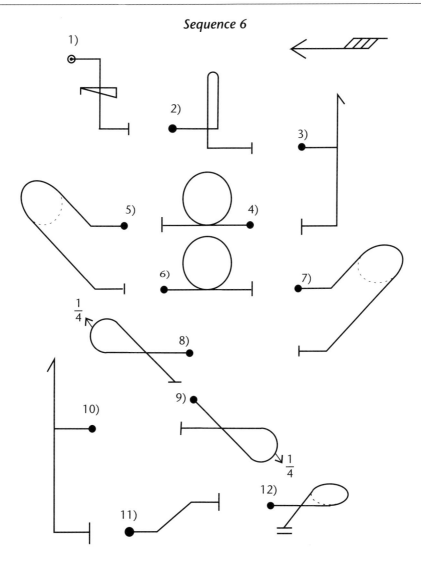

1) 1 Turn Erect Spin (k=14)
2) Canopy Down Humpty-
   Bump (k=13)
3) Stall Turn (k=17)
4) Loop (k=10)
5) Chandelle (k=12)
6) Loop (k=10)

7) Chandelle (k=12)
8) Quarter Cloverleaf (k=16)
9) Quarter Cloverleaf (k=16)
10) Stall Turn (k=17)
11) 45° Up-Line (k=7)
12) 270° Turn (k=5)

Overall k = 149

ABOVE: A Lö 100 in a 45° Down-Line. (*Mike Woollard*)
LEFT: A unique view of the Fox in an inverted turn. (*J. Ewald*)

## Sequence 7

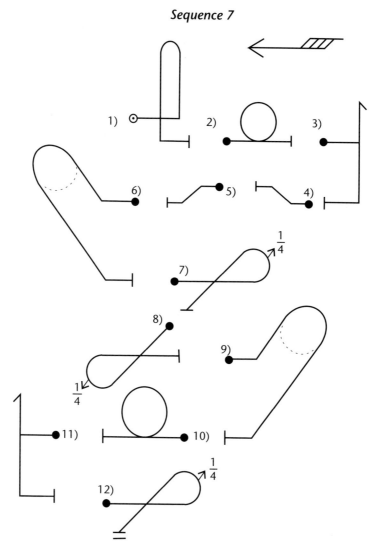

1) Canopy Down Humpty-
   Bump (k=13)
2) Loop (k=10)
3) Stall Turn (k=17)
4) 45° Up-Line (k=7)
5) 45° Down-Line (k=7)
6) Chandelle (k=12)

7) Quarter Cloverleaf (k=16)
8) Quarter Cloverleaf (k=16)
9) Chandelle (k=12)
10) Loop (k=10)
11) Stall Turn (k=17)
12) Quarter Cloverleaf (k=16)

Overall k = 153

## Sequence 8

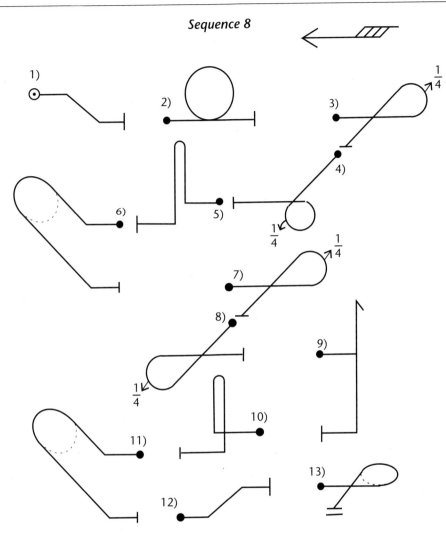

1) 45° Down-Line (k=7)
2) Loop (k=10)
3) Quarter Cloverleaf (k=16)
4) Quarter Cloverleaf (k=16)
5) Canopy Up Humpty-
   Bump (k=15)
6) Chandelle (k=12)
7) Quarter Cloverleaf (k=16)

8) Quarter Cloverleaf (k=16)
9) Stall Turn (k=17)
10) Canopy Down Humpty-
   Bump (k=13)
11) Chandelle (k=12)
12) 45° Up-Line (k=7)
13) 270° Turn (k=5)

Overall k = 162

ABOVE:  Views from the Fox at similar speeds in inverted and horizontal flight. Note the dramatically different attitudes in each case. *(Mike Woollard)*
OPPOSITE:  Views of rolling from inverted to erect flight. *(Mike Woollard)*

## Sequence 9

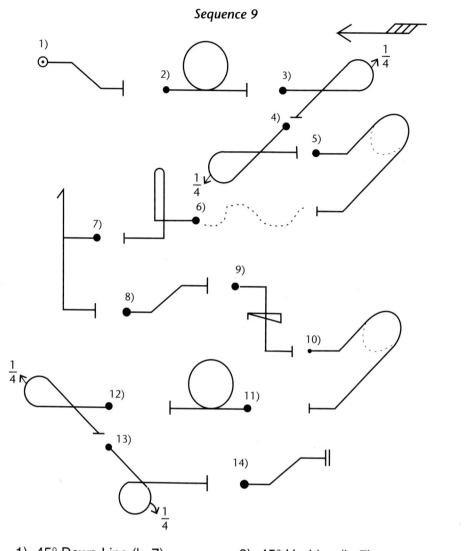

1) 45° Down-Line (k=7)
2) Loop (k=10)
3) Quarter Cloverleaf (k=16)
4) Quarter Cloverleaf (k=16)
5) Chandelle (k=12)
6) Canopy Down Humpty-
   Bump (k=13)
7) Stall Turn (k=17)

8) 45° Up-Line (k=7)
9) 1 Turn Spin (k=14)
10) Chandelle (k=12)
11) Loop (k=10)
12) Quarter Cloverleaf (k=16)
13) Quarter Cloverleaf (k=16)
14) 45° Up-Line (k=7)

Overall k = 173

## Sequence 10

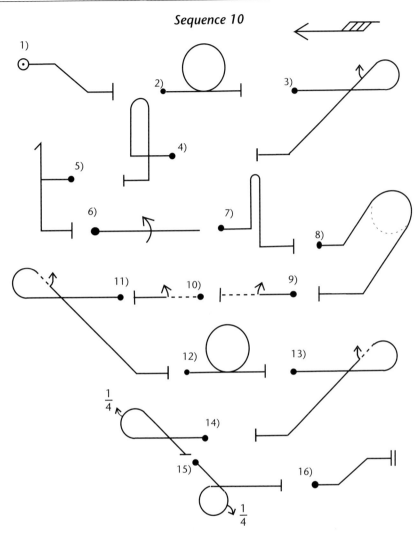

1) 45° Down-Line (k=7)
2) Loop (k=10)
3) Half Cuban Eight (k=16)
4) Canopy Down Humpty-Bump (k=13)
5) Stall Turn (k=17)
6) Full Slow Roll (k=14)
7) Canopy Up Humpty-Bump (k=15)
8) Chandelle (k=12)
9) Half Roll to Inverted (k=8)
10) Half Roll to Erect (k=8)
11) Half Cuban Eight (k=16)
12) Loop (k=10)
13) Half Cuban Eight (k=16)
14) Quarter Cloverleaf (k=16)
15) Quarter Cloverleaf (k=16)
16) 45° Up-Line (k=7)

Overall k = 201

# Appendix

## Draw Your Own Flight Envelope

**A** very interesting exercise and a useful prerequisite to aerobatics in a new type of glider is to draw out the Flight Envelope. Ideally, it should be to the same scale as any envelopes drawn for other gliders to enable a comparison to be made. Such a comparison is graphically illustrated in Fig 3 where the envelopes for the Swift, K6e, K21, Fox, Pilatus B4 and the Puchacz can be seen to be dramatically different from each other.

Start by preparing a graph with the vertical axis sub-divided in +ve and -ve **g** values of load factor between -10 and +10. The horizontal axis is equally sub-divided to cover an airspeed range from zero to a conveniently high value such as 180 knots.

The flight manual should be consulted for the relevant speeds and load conditions which can then be plotted on the graph. If not all the information is provided, as is often the case, it will be necessary to consult either the manufacturers or other aerobatic pilots with experience of the particular type. Plot the key points on the graph, joining them together in the order given below to form the Flight Envelope as shown in Fig 2.

(a) The intersection of the zero load line with the **1g** erect stall speed line.

(b) Erect stall speed at **1g** positive loading, point 'b'.

(c) Max manoeuvring speed $V_a$ at the maximum +Ve **g** load factor for the glider $n$, point 'c'.
**NB:** Points 'b' and 'c' are joined by a quadratic curve which strictly speaking has the shape:

At any velocity V, the Load Factor $n =$

$$\frac{(n_1-1)(V^2-V_s^2)}{(V_a^2-V_s^2)} +1$$

but an approximate curve drawn between these points of the shape as shown in Fig 2 will suffice.

(d) Max rough airspeed $V_b$ where it falls along line c-e, i.e. Point 'd' (NB: As Fig 2 shows, whilst this is not strictly correct, for all practical purposes it is a reasonable approximation.)

(e) Point 'e', the velocity never exceed speed in erect flight $V_{ne}$ at the equivalent load factor $n$ if quoted in the manual, otherwise use a load factor of $(n_1-\frac{1}{4}g)$ the reduction of $\frac{1}{4}g$ reflecting the loss of wing strength which occurs with speed between $V_a$ and $V_{ne}$. (NB: The $V_{ne}$ maximum load factor $n_2$ should be given in the flight manual if it is significantly different to $n_2$ at $V_a$.

(f) $V_{ne}$ at a load factor of zero, point 'f'.

(g) $V'_{ne}$ at the equivalent load factor $n_3$ if quoted in the manual, otherwise use the maximum inverted load factor $n_4$ reduced by $\frac{1}{4}g$ to reflect the fall in wing strength with speed, point 'g'.

(h) Max inverted manoeuvring speed in inverted flight $V'_a$ at the maximum inverted load factor $n_4$, point 'h'.
(NB: Usually $V_a$ and $V'_a$ are the same)

(i) Max rough air speed $V'_b$ at a slightly increased maximum inverted load factor (if not quoted use $-V_b$) positioned where it falls along line g-i, point 'h'.

(j) Inverted stalling speed $V'_s$ at a load factor of -1g, point 'j'. **NB:** As between points 'b' and 'c' the points 'i' and 'j' are joined by a quadratic curve which again can be drawn approximately as illustrated in Fig 2.

(k)   The intersection of the zero load line with the $-1g$ inverted stall speed line.

(l)   Points 'b' and 'j' should be extended to the origin point 'o' thereby completing the envelope.

(m)   A horizontal line m-n between the boundaries of the flight envelope at a load factor $+3\frac{1}{2}g$ should be drawn to represent the maximum load factor allowable when airbrakes are deployed.

(n)   Line p-q and r-s between the boundaries of the Flight Envelope drawn parallel to c-e and g-i respectively but at one third of the load factor magnitude, to represent the maximum load factor allowable when using aileron (full aileron at $V_a$ or ⅓rd aileron deflection at $V_{ne}$).

## References and Additional Reading

Reference 1    Irvin and Welch, *New Soaring Pilot*, 3rd Edition 1977 Chap 20.

Reference 2    Royal Air Force, *Principles of Flight*, 1983, p10

Reference 3    MoD. Defence Standards 00-970, Design and Airworthiness Requirements for Service Aircraft, Vol 1 – Aeroplanes. 203/1.

Reference 4    Airworthiness Steering Committee. Joint Airworthiness Requirements JAR22 Sailplanes and Powered Sailplanes, Change 4, 7 May 1987. Originated 1 April 1980.

Reference 5    Neil Williams, *Aerobatics* Airlife Publishing, ISBN  0950454303 Chandelles and wing-over definitions – Chapter 28

Reference 6    Eric Müller & Annette Carson, *Flight Unlimited* p36. Eastern Press. 1983

Reference 7    Fédération Aéronautique Internationale Aerobatics Commission (CIVA). Regulations for the conduct of International Aerobatic Events Part Two. Events for Glider Aircraft 1993 incl Amendment No: 1 - 1 Jan 1993

# Index